SpringerBriefs in Computer Science

For other titles published in this series, go to
www.springer.com/series/10028

Angelos D. Keromytis

Voice over IP Security

A Comprehensive Survey of Vulnerabilities
and Academic Research

Angelos D. Keromytis
Department of Computer Science
Mail Code 0401
Columbia University
1214 Amsterdam Avenue
10027 New York
USA
angelos@cs.columbia.edu

ISSN 2191-5768   e-ISSN 2191-5776
ISBN 978-1-4419-9865-1   e-ISBN 978-1-4419-9866-8
DOI 10.1007/978-1-4419-9866-8
Springer New York Dordrecht Heidelberg London

Library of Congress Control Number: 2011926000

Printed on acid-free paper

Springer is part of Springer Science+Business Media (www.springer.com)

To the four women in my life: Elizabeth, Penelope, Julia and Sia. And to my dad, Dennis.

Preface

When I decided to do a sabbatical with Symantec Research Labs Europe in the beautiful French Riviera, I was asked to work on a project about Voice over IP (VoIP) security. The goal of the VAMPIRE Project[1] was to understand the threats and vulnerabilities of VoIP systems, and to inform the direction of further research efforts. Although I was interested in this problem space, I only knew the subject from the point of view of a security researcher who has not studied VoIP itself in any great depth. As such, this project served as an ideal vehicle in educating me about VoIP security.

This book is the result of more than 18 months' work to learn what the challenges and opportunities are in securing VoIP. It is primarily addressed to students and researchers who want to learn about VoIP security, and is meant as both an introduction to the problem space and an extensive reference to related work as of early 2011. It is also intended as a case study on how to approach and map out a new research area.

The structure of this book reflects my learning process. We start by learning the lay of the land (Overview of VoIP Systems). We then proceed to find out what *actual* problems are encountered by VoIP systems by looking at reported vulnerabilities (Survey and Analysis of VoIP/IMS Vulnerabilities). Finally, we explore as much of the prior work in this space as I could find (Survey of VoIP Security Research Literature). The book concludes with some comparative analysis and practical recommendations for securing VoIP systems and infrastructures.

This work would not have been possible but for the support of several people. I would like to thank Marc Dacier, not only for arranging and managing my sabbatical at Symantec, but also for being a great colleague and friend. Thanks to Corrado Leita for sharing his office with me during that time, serving as a listening board, offering thoughtful suggestions, and generally putting up with me. Thanks to Susan

---

[1] The project was funded by the Agence Nationale de la Recherche, the French equivalent of the U.S. National Science Foundation. The overall effort was led by INRIA Nancy, with Eurecom, Orange Labs, and Symantec Research Labs Europe as partners. See http://vampire.gforge.inria.fr/ for more details.

Lagerstrom-Fife, Jennifer Evans and Jennifer Maurer at Springer for suggesting this project and making the process easy.

Finally, thanks to my wife, Elizabeth, and two daughters, Penelope and Julia, for tolerating my work schedule and quirkiness during (and before) the conduct of the work and the authoring of this book[2]. I'm sure you'll have to put up with me afterwards too!

New York, 14 February 2011   *Angelos D. Keromytis*

---

[2] For example, note the date of this foreword. Whoever writes a preface at 1am on Valentine's Day?

Contents

Acronyms xi

1 Introduction 1
   1.1 Motivation and Background 1
   1.2 What This Book is About 3
        1.2.1 Organization 4

2 Overview of VoIP Systems 5
   2.1 Session Initiation Protocol 6
   2.2 Unlicensed Mobile Access 10
   2.3 Other VoIP Systems 11

3 Survey and Analysis of VoIP/IMS Vulnerabilities 13
   3.1 Survey of Disclosed Vulnerabilities 16
   3.2 Analysis of the Vulnerability Survey 20

4 Survey of VoIP Security Research Literature 27
   4.1 Collection Methodology 27
   4.2 Extended VoIPSA Classification 28
   4.3 Survey of VoIP Security Research 29
        4.3.1 VoIPSA-based Classification (111 items) 29
        4.3.2 Additional Categories (134 items) 44

5 Comparative Analysis 57
   5.1 Recommendations for Securing VoIP Systems 59

6 Conclusions 61

References 63

Acronyms

3DES	Triple DES
AES	Advanced Encryption Standard
BER	Bit Error Rate
CBR	Constant Bit Rate
COTS	Commercial Off-The-Shelf
CSRF	Cross Site Request Forgery; also XSRF
CVE	Common Vulnerabilities and Exposures
DES	Data Encryption Standard
DHCP	Dynamic Host Configuration Protocol
DNS	Domain Name System
DoS	Denial of Service
DTLS	Datagram Transport Layer Security (protocol)
EAP	Extensible Authentication Protocol
ECDH	Elliptic Curve Diffie Hellman
ECDSA	Elliptic Curve Digital Signature Algorithm
FTP	File Transfer Protocol
GSM	Global System for Mobile Communications; originally Groupe Spcial Mobile
IDS	Intrusion Detection System
IETF	Internet Engineering Task Force
IM	Instant Messaging
IMS	Internet Multimedia Subsystem
IPsec	IP Security (protocol)
ITU	International Telecommunications Union
NAT	Network Address Translation
P2P	Peer-to-Peer
PBX	Private Branch Exchange
PKI	Public Key Infrastructure
PPPoE	Point-to-Point Protocol over Ethernet
PSTN	Public Switched Telephony Network
QoS	Quality of Service

RFC   Request For Comments
RTP   Real Time Protocol
S/MIME   Secure/Multipurpose Internet Mail Extensions
SDP   Session Description Protocol
SIP   Session Initiation Protocol
SMS   Short Messaging Service
SOHO   Small Office Home Office
SPIM   SPam over Instant Messaging
SPIT   SPam over Internet Telephony
SQL   Structured Query Language
TCP   Transmission Control Protocol
TFTP   Trivial File Transfer Protocol
TLS   Transport Layer Security (protocol)
UDP   User Datagram Protocol
UMA   Unlicensed Mobile Access
UMTS   Universal Mobile Telecommunications System
uPnP   Universal Plug-and-Play
VBR   Variable Bit Rate
VoIP   Voice over IP
VoIPSA   VoIP Security Alliance
XSS   Cross Site Scripting
XSRF   See CSRF

Abstract Voice over IP (VoIP) and Internet Multimedia Subsystem technologies (IMS) are rapidly being adopted by consumers, enterprises, governments and militaries. These technologies offer higher flexibility and more features than traditional telephony (PSTN) infrastructures, as well as the potential for lower cost through equipment consolidation and, for the consumer market, new business models. However, VoIP systems also represent a higher complexity in terms of architecture, protocols and implementation, with a corresponding increase in the potential for misuse.

In this book, we examine the current state of affairs on VoIP security through a survey of 221 known/disclosed security vulnerabilities in bug-tracking databases. We complement this with a comprehensive survey of the state of the art in VoIP security research that covers 245 papers. Juxtaposing our findings, we identify current areas of risk and deficiencies in research focus. This book should serve as a starting point for understanding the threats and risks in a rapidly evolving set of technologies that are seeing increasing deployment and use. An additional goal is to gain a better understanding of the security landscape with respect to VoIP toward directing future research in this and other similar emerging technologies.

Key words: VoIP, SIP, security, vulnerabilities, attacks, literature

1
Introduction

1.1 Motivation and Background

The rate at which new technologies are being introduced and adopted by society has been steadily accelerating throughout human history. The advent of pervasive computing and telecommunications has reinforced this trend. In this environment of constant innovation, individuals, governments and organizations have been struggling to manage the tension between reaping the benefits of new technologies while understanding and managing their risks. In this struggle, cost reductions, convenience and new features typically overcome security concerns. As a result, security experts (but also the government and the courts of law) are often left with the task of playing "catch up" with those who exploit flaws to further their own goals. This is the situation we find ourselves in with respect to one popular class of technologies, collectively referred to as Voice over IP (VoIP).

VoIP refers to a class of products that enable advanced communication services over data networks. While voice is a key aspect in such products, video and other capabilities (e.g., collaborative editing and whiteboard sharing, file sharing, calendaring) are supported. The key advantages of VoIP are flexibility and low cost. The former derives from the (generally) open architectures and software-based implementation, while the latter is due to new business models, equipment and network-link consolidation, and ubiquitous consumer-grade broadband connectivity.

Due to these benefits, VoIP has seen rapid uptake in both the enterprise and consumer markets. An increasing number of enterprises are replacing their internal phone switches with VoIP-based implementations, both to introduce new features and to eliminate redundant equipment. Consumers have embraced a slew of technologies with different features and costs, including P2P calling (e.g., Skype), Internet-to-PSTN network bridging, and wireless VoIP. These new technologies and business models are being promoted by a new generation of startup companies that are challenging the traditional status quo in telephony and personal telecommunications. As a result, a number of PSTN providers have already completed or are in the process of transitioning from circuit-switched networks to VoIP-friendly packet-switched backbones. Finally, as the commercial and consumer sectors go, so do governments and militaries due to cost reduction concerns and the general dependence on Commercial Off The Shelf (COTS) equipment for the majority of their computing needs.

However, higher complexity is often the price we pay for more flexibility. In the case of VoIP technologies, a number of factors contribute to architectural, protocol, implementation and operational complexity:

- The number and complexity of the various features integrated in a product are perhaps the single largest source of complexity. For example, voice and video transmission typically allow for a variety of codecs which may be used in almost-arbitrary combinations. Since one of the biggest selling points for VoIP is feature-richness and the desire to unify personal communications under the same umbrella, this is a particularly pertinent concern.
- Openness and modularity, generally considered desirable traits, allow for a number of independent implementations and products. Each of these comes with its own parameters and design choices. Interoperability concerns and customer feedback then lead to an ever-growing baseline of supported features for all products. A compounding factor to increasing complexity for many of the open VoIP protocols is the "design-by-committee" syndrome, which typically leads to larger, more inclusive specifications than would otherwise be the case (e.g., in a closed, proprietary environment such as the wireline telephony network from 20 years ago).
- Because VoIP systems are envisioned to operate in a variety of environments, business settings, and network conditions, they must offer considerable configurability, which in turns leads to high complexity. Of particular concern are unforeseen feature interactions and other emergent properties.
- Finally, VoIP are generally meant to work over a public data network (e.g., the Internet), or an enterprise/operator network that uses the same underlying technology. As a result, there is a substantial amount of (strictly speaking) non-VoIP infrastructure that is critical for the correct operation of the system, including such protocols/services as DHCP [69], DNS [170, 171], TFTP/BOOTP [86, 240], NAT [245] (and NAT traversal protocols such as STUN [213]), NTP [169], SNMP [119], routing, the web (HTTP [31, 85], TLS/SSL [64], etc.) and many others. As we shall see, even a "perfectly secure" VoIP system can be compromised by subverting elements of this infrastructure.

Because of the need to seamlessly interoperate with the existing telephony infrastructure, the new features, and the speed of development and deployment, VoIP protocols and products have been repeatedly found to contain numerous vulnerabilities [136, 137, 138] that have been exploited [143, 255, 256]. As a result, a fair amount of research has been directed towards addressing some of these issues. However, the effort is unbalanced, with little effort spent on some highly deserving problem areas.

As a result of this complexity, which manifests itself both in terms of configuration options and size of the code base for VoIP implementations, VoIP systems represent a very large attack surface. Thus, one should expect to encounter, over time, security problems arising from design flaws (e.g., exploitable protocol weaknesses), undesirable feature interactions (e.g., combinations of components that make new attacks possible or existing/known attacks easier), unforeseen dependencies (e.g., compromise paths through seemingly unrelated protocols), weak configurations, and, not least, implementation flaws.

1.2 What This Book is About

In this manuscript, we attempt a first effort at mapping out the space of VoIP threats and risks, and comparing it with the state of the art in security research.

We begin by conducting a survey of the "actually seen" vulnerabilities and attacks, as reported by the popular press and by bug-tracking databases. In trying to understand the threat space against VoIP, our approach is to place known vulnerabilities within a structured framework. While a single taxonomy is not likely to be definitive, using several different viewpoints and mapping the vulnerability space along several axis may reveal trends and areas that merit further analysis. As a starting point, we use the taxonomy provided by the Voice over IP Security Alliance (VoIPSA), available at http://www.voipsa.org/. VoIPSA is a vendor-neutral, not-for-profit organization composed of VoIP and security vendors, organizations and individuals with an interest in securing VoIP protocols, products and installations. The classification uses 6 broad areas of concern: (1) social threats, (2) traffic eavesdropping, interception and modification threats, (3) denial of service (DoS), (4) service abuse, (5) physical access threats, and (6) interruption of services threats. Due to the nature of the vulnerabilities discussed, only the first 4 categories are relevant to our discussion. we also place the surveyed vulnerabilities within the traditional threat space of confidentiality, integrity, availability (CIA), and consider whether the vulnerabilities exploit bugs in the protocol, implementation or system configuration.

We also conduct a second comprehensive survey that covers 245 VoIP security research papers and books. Our primary goal here is to create a roadmap of existing work in securing VoIP, towards reducing the start-up effort required by other researchers to initiate research in this space. A secondary goal is to identify gaps in existing research, and to help inform the security community of challenges and opportunities for further work. Finally, we seek to provide guidance as to what further work in needed to better understand and analyze the activities of attackers. We classify these papers according to the class of threat they seek to address, using an extended version of the VoIP Security Alliance (VoIPSA) [264] threat taxonomy. We discuss our findings, and contrast them with the previous survey on VoIP vulnerabilities.

1.2.1 Organization

The remainder of this book is organized as follows. Section 2 contains an overview of two major VoIP technologies, SIP and UMA. While we refer to other VoIP systems throughout the discussion, we focus on the specific two technologies as they are both representative, widely used, and well-documented. In Sec. 3 we discuss VoIP threats and place known attacks against VoIP systems within the taxonomy proposed by the VoIP Security Alliance. We then present our survey of the VoIP security research literature in Sec. 4. Section 5 compares the findings of the two surveys. Informed by the two surveys, we discuss the current state of VoIP security, we provide practical recommendations for securing VoIP systems and infrastructures. We conclude by discussing possible future directions for security research and practices in Sec. 6.

2
Overview of VoIP Systems

In their simplest form, Voice over IP protocols simply enable two (or more) devices to transmit and receive real-time audio traffic that allows their respective users to communicate. In general, VoIP architectures are partitioned in two main components: signaling and media transfer. Signaling covers both abstract notions, such as endpoint naming and addressing, and concrete protocol functions such as parameter negotiation, access control, billing, proxying, and NAT traversal. Depending on the architecture, quality of service (QoS) and device configuration/management may also be part of the signaling protocol (or protocol family). The media transfer aspect of VoIP systems generally includes a comparatively simpler protocol for encapsulating data, with support for multiple codecs and (often, but not always) content security. A commonly used media transfer protocol is RTP [219]. There exits an RTP profile (named Secure RTP, or SRTP [131]) that supports encryption and integrity protection, but it is not yet widely used. The RTP protocol family also includes RTCP, which is used to control certain RTP parameters between communicating endpoints.

However, a variety of other features are generally also desired by users and offered by providers as a means for differentiation by competing technologies and services, such video, integration with calendaring and file sharing, and bridging to other networks (*e.g.,* to the "regular" telephony network). Furthermore, a number of different decisions may be made when designing a VoIP system, reflecting different requirements and approaches to addressing, billing, mobility, security and access control, usability, and other issues. Consequently, there exist a variety of different VoIP protocols and architectures. For concreteness, we will focus our attention on a popular and widely deployed technology: the Session Initiation Protocol (SIP) [212]. We will also discuss the Unlicensed Mobile Access (UMA) architecture [1], as a different approach to VoIP that is gaining traction among wireless telephony operators. In the rest of this chapter, we give a high-level overview of SIP and UMA, followed by a brief description of the salient points of a few other popular VoIP systems, such as H.323 and Skype. We will refer back to this overview when discussing the threat space and specific vulnerabilities in Sec. 3.

2.1 Session Initiation Protocol

SIP is a protocol standardized by the Internet Engineering Task Force (IETF), and is designed to support the setup of bidirectional communication sessions including, but not limited to, VoIP calls. It is similar in some ways to HTTP, in that it is text-based, has a request-response structure, and even uses a mechanism based on the HTTP Digest Authentication [88] for user authentication. However, it is an inherently stateful protocol that supports interaction with multiple network components (e.g., middleboxes such as PSTN bridges), and asynchronous notifications. While its finite state machine is seemingly simple, in practice it has become quite large and complicated — an observation supported by the fact that the main SIP RFC [212] is one of the longest ever defined (after the encyclopedic "Internet Security Glossary" RFC 4949), with additional RFCs further extending the specification. Figure 1 shows the number of SIP-related RFCs (and the number of total bytes in these) per year (until May 2009), and a size comparison of the main SIP RFC with respect to the TCP RFC, the 5 main MIME RFCs, the 2 Secure MIME (S/MIME) RFCs, and the 4 main IPsec RFCs. These graphs should provide a quantitative, if indirect, indication of the complexity of SIP.

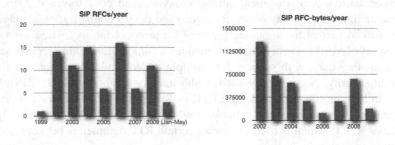

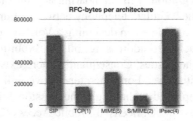

Fig. 1 Breakdown of SIP-related RFCs and their sizes

SIP can operate over a number of transport protocols, including TCP [190], UDP [189] and SCTP [179]. UDP is generally the preferred method due to simplicity

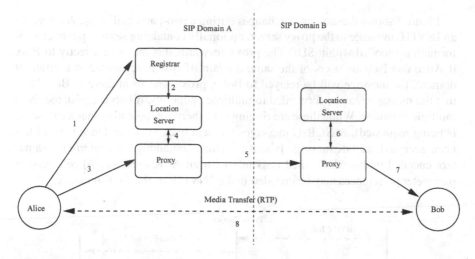

Fig. 2 Session Initiation Protocol (SIP) entity interactions. User Alice registers with her domain's Registrar (1), which stores the information in the Location Server (2). When placing a call, Alice contacts her local Proxy Server (3), which may consult the Location Server (4). A call may be forwarded to another Proxy Server (5), which will consult its domain Location Server (6) before forwarding the call to the final recipient. After the SIP negotiation terminates, RTP is used directly between Alice and Bob to transfer media content. For simplicity, this diagram does not show the possible interaction between Alice and a Redirection Server (which would, in turn, interact with the Location Server).

and performance, although TCP has the advantage of supporting TLS protection of call setup. However, recent work on Datagram TLS (DTLS) [205] may render this irrelevant. SCTP, on the other hand, offers several advantages over both TCP and UDP, including DoS resistance [114], multi-homing and mobility support, and logical connection multiplexing over a single channel.

In the SIP architecture, the main entities are end points (whether softphones or physical devices), a proxy server, a registrar, a redirect server, and a location server. Figure 2 shows a high-level view of the SIP entity interactions. The registrar, proxy and redirect servers may be combined, or they may be separate entities operated independently. Endpoints communicate with a registrar to indicate their presence. This information is stored in the location server. A user may be registered via multiple endpoints simultaneously.

During call setup, the endpoint communicates with the proxy which uses the location server to determine where the call should be routed to. This may be another endpoint in the same network (e.g., within the same enterprise), or another proxy server in another network. Alternatively, endpoints may use a redirect server to directly determine where a call should be directed to; redirect servers consult with the location server in the same way that proxy servers operate during call setup. Once an end-to-end channel has been established (through one or more proxies) between the two endpoints, SIP negotiates the actual session parameters (such as the codecs, RTP ports, etc.) using the Session Description Protocol (SDP) [113].

Figure 3 shows the message exchanges during a two-party call setup. Alice sends an INVITE message to the proxy server, optionally containing session parameter information encoded within SDP. The proxy forwards this message directly to Bob, if Alice and Bob are users of the same domain. If Bob is registered in a different domain, the message will be relayed to Bob's proxy, and from there to Bob. Note that the message may be forwarded to multiple endpoints, if bob is registered from multiple locations. While these are ringing (or otherwise indicating that a call setup is being requested), RINGING messages are sent back to Alice. Once the call has been accepted, an OK message is sent to Alice, containing his preferred parameters encoded within SDP. Alice responds with an ACK message. Alice's session parameter preferences may be encoded in the INVITE or the ACK message.

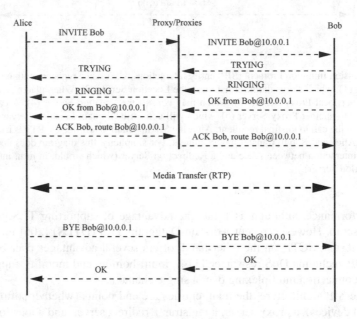

Fig. 3 Message exchanges during a SIP-based two-party call setup.

Following this exchange, the two endpoints can begin transmitting voice, video or other content (as negotiated) using the agreed-upon media transport protocol, typically RTP. While the signaling traffic may be relayed through a number of SIP proxies, the media traffic is exchanged directly between the two endpoints. When bridging different networks, e.g., PSTN and SIP, media gateways may disrupt the end-to-end nature of the media transfer. These entities translate content (e.g., audio) between the formats that are supported by the different networks.

Because signaling and media transfer operate independent of each other, the endpoints are responsible for indicating to the proxies that the call has been terminated, using a BYE message which is relayed through the proxies along the same path as the call setup messages.

There are many other protocol interactions supported by SIP, that cover many common (and uncommon) scenarios including call forwarding (manual or automatic), conference calling, voicemail, etc. Typically, this is done by semantically overloading SIP messages such that they can play various roles in different parts of the call. We shall see in Sec. 3 examples of how this flexibility and protocol modularity can be used to attack the system. It is worth pointing out that many of the vulnerabilities we will discuss in Sec. 3 are at least partially caused by this complexity. Some efforts to formally define and analyze parts of the protocol have pointed out subtle problems [285], but such efforts have not (yet) been extended to cover significant portions of the specifications due to their size and complexity.

All SIP traffic is typically transmitted over port 5060 (UDP or TCP), although that is configurable. The ports used for the media traffic, however, are dynamic and negotiated via SDP during call setup. This poses some problems when Network Address Translation (NAT) or firewalls are traversed. Typically, these have to be stateful and understand the SIP exchanges so that they can open the appropriate RTP ports for the media transfer. In the case of NAT traversal, endpoints may use protocols like STUN to enable communication. Alternatively, the Universal Plug-and-Play (uPnP) protocol [1] may be used in some environments, such as residential broadband networks consisting of a single subnet behind a NAT gateway.

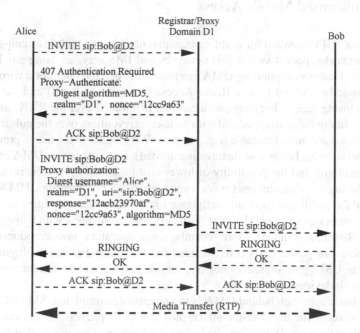

Fig. 4 SIP Digest Authentication

---

[1] http://www.upnp.org/

For authenticating endpoints, the registrar and the proxy typically use HTTP Digest Authentication, as shown in Fig. 4. This is a simple challenge-response protocol that uses a shared secret key along with a username, domain name, a nonce, and specific fields from the SIP message to compute a cryptographic hash. Using this mechanism, passwords are not transmitted in plaintext form over the network. It is worth noting that authentication may be requested at almost any point during a call setup. We shall later see an example where this can be abused by a malicious party to conduct toll fraud in some environments.

For more complex authentication scenarios, SIP can use S/MIME encapsulation [196] to carry complex payloads, including public keys and certificates. When TCP is used as the transport protocol for SIP, TLS can be used to protect the SIP messages. TLS is required for communication among proxies, registrars and redirect servers, but only recommended between endpoints and proxies or registrars. Alternatively, IPsec [135] may be used to protect all communications, regardless of the transport protocol. However, because few implementations integrate SIP, RTP and IPsec, it is left to system administrators to figure out how to setup and manage such configurations.

2.2 Unlicensed Mobile Access

UMA is a 3GPP standard for enabling transparent access to mobile circuit-switched voice networks, packet-switch data networks and IMS services using any IP-based substrate. Handsets supporting UMA can roam between the operator's wireless network (usually referred to as a Radio Access Network, or RAN) and the Internet without losing access. For example, a call that is initiated over the RAN can then be routed, without being dropped and with no user intervention, over the public Internet if conditions are more favorable (e.g., stronger WiFi signal in the user's premises, or in a hotel wireless hotspot while traveling abroad). For consumers, UMA offers better connectivity and the possibility of lower cost by enabling new business models and reducing roaming charges (under some scenarios). For operators, UMA reduces the need for additional spectrum, cellphone towers and related equipment. A variety of cellphones supporting UMA over WiFi currently exist, along with home gateways and USB-stick softphones. More recently, some operators have introduced femtocells (ultra-low power RAN cells intended for consumer-directed deployment) that can act as UMA gateways, allowing any mobile handset to take advantage of UMA where such devices are deployed.

The basic approach behind UMA is to encapsulate complete GSM and 3G radio frames (except for the over-the-air crypto) inside IP packets. These can then be transmitted over any IP network, including the Internet. This means that the mobile operator can continue to use the existing back-end equipment; all that is needed is a gateway that decapsulates the GSM/3G frames and injects them to the existing circuit-switched network (for voice calls), as can be seen in Fig. 5.

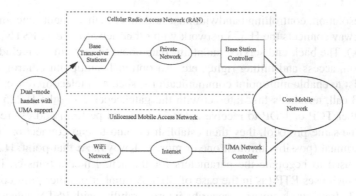

Fig. 5 Unlicensed Mobile Access (UMA) conceptual architecture

To protect both signaling and media traffic confidentiality and integrity while traversing untrusted (and untrustworthy) networks, UMA uses IPsec. All traffic between the handset (or, more generally, UMA endpoint) and the provider's UMA Network Controller (or a firewall/VPN concentrator screening traffic) is encrypted and integrity-protected using ESP [134]. The use of IPsec provides a high level of security for the traffic, once keys and other parameters have been negotiated. For that purpose, the IKEv2 key management protocol [133] is used. Authentication uses the EAP-SIM [120] (for GSM handsets) and EAP-AKA [18] (for UMTS handsets) profiles. Authentication is asymmetric: the provider authenticates to the handset using digital signatures and public key certificates, while the handset authenticates using a SIM-embedded secret key. It is worth pointing out that UMA provides stronger authentication guarantees than the baseline cellphone network, in that the provider does not authenticate to the handset in a RAN. Furthermore, the cryptographic algorithms used in IPsec (AES and 3DES) are considered significantly stronger than the on-the-air algorithms used in GSM.

Despite the use of strong cryptography and sound protocols, UMA introduces some new risks in the operator networks, since these now have to be connected to the public Internet in a much more intimate fashion. In particular, the security gateway must process IPsec traffic, including the relatively complex IKEv2 protocol, and a number of UMA-related discovery and configuration protocols. These increase the attack surface and overall security exposure of the operators significantly.

2.3 Other VoIP Systems

H.323 is an ITU-defined protocol family for VoIP (audio and video) over packet-switched data networks. The various subprotocols are encoded in ASN.1 format. In the H.323 world, the main entities are terminals (software or physical phones), a gateway, a gatekeeper and a back-end service. The gatekeeper is responsible for address resolution, controlling bandwidth use and other management functions, while the gateway connects the H.323 network with other networks (*e.g.*, PSTN, or a SIP network). The back-end service maintains data about the terminals, including configuration, access and billing rights, etc. An optional multipoint control unit may also exist to enable multipoint communications, such as a teleconference. To setup a H.323 call, terminals first interact with the gatekeeper using the H.225 protocol over either TCP or UDP to receive authorization and perform address resolution. Using the same protocol, they then establish the end-to-end connection to the remote terminal (possibly through one or more gateways). At that point, H.245 over TCP is used to negotiate the parameters for the actual media transfer, including ports, which uses RTP (as in the case of SIP). A number of other protocols within the H.323 framework covering security, interoperability with PSTN, teleconferencing, and others. Authentication may be requested at several steps during call setup, and typically depends on symmetric keys but may also use digital signatures. Voice encryption is also supported through SRTP and MIKEY [19]. Unlike SIP, H.323 does not use a well-known port, making firewall traversal even more complicated.

Skype[2] is a peer-to-peer VoIP system that was originally available as a softphone for desktop computers but has since been integrated into cellphones and other handheld devices, either as an add-on or as the exclusive communication mechanism. It offers voice, video, and text messaging to all other Skype users free of charge, and provides bridging (typically for a fee) to the PSTN both for outgoing and incoming calls and text messages (SMS). The underlying protocol is proprietary, and the software itself incorporates several anti-reverse engineering techniques. Nonetheless, some analysis [26, 32] and reverse engineering [38] have taken place, indicating both the ubiquitous use of strong cryptography and the presence of some software bugs (at the time of the work). The system uses a centralized login server but is otherwise fully distributed with respect to intra-Skype communications.

A number of chat (IM) networks, such as the AOL Instant Messenger, Microsoft's Live Messenger, Yahoo! Messenger, and Google Talk offer voice and video capabilities as well. Although each network uses its own (often proprietary) protocol, there exist bridges between most of them, allowing inter-IM communication at the text level. In most of these networks, users can place outgoing voice calls to the PSTN. Some popular IM clients also integrate SIP support.

---

[2] http://www.skype.com/

3
Survey and Analysis of VoIP/IMS Vulnerabilities

VoIP systems, being primarily software-based, suffer from all the usual vulnerabilities that plague other applications, such as buffer overflows [14] and application-level denial of service [56]. Nonetheless, several additional factors make VoIP a particularly interesting environment from a security perspective:

- *Scale and complexity:* VoIP infrastructures include more than just the bare protocols needed for voice/video transfer. They depend on pretty much all known protocols for their correct operation. These include (but are not limited to) DNS, web technologies, NAT, TFTP, DHCP/PPPoE, network quality of service, firewalls, etc. Consequently, VoIP infrastructures present a very large attack surface and inherit the network and implementation vulnerabilities of each of their components.
  Furthermore, the (often haphazard) composition of these elements results in *emergent properties*. These are possible system behaviors that are not part of the system design and often represent security vulnerabilities. One representative example of such properties (discussed below) is the possibility of Cross-Site Scripting (XSS) attacks to the web-based management interface for VoIP phones through poisoned content stored in the call log database of the device; said content was placed in the database by direct manipulation of SIP fields.
- *Billing infrastructure:* VoIP systems are typically offered by a commercial provider, which also operates a billing infrastructure that is tightly integrated with the operational side. Thus, vulnerabilities in VoIP systems can sometimes lead to immediate monetization (e.g., through toll fraud or phantom refunds). Additionally, miscreants can leverage this infrastructure to siphon away funds or exfiltrate them through inter-provider payments or other legitimate mechanisms available through the billing infrastructure. This is a major difference with most other types of online criminal activity, which typically requires both a system compromise and a subsequent exploitation, with the two requiring very different technical means (e.g., contrast with phishing, spamming, or credential stealing through key loggers).

- *User expectations:* Because VoIP users associate these mechanisms with PSTN services, they are used to paying for actions they take. The charges may be for small amounts, but there are often many of them in each billing cycle. This would make it easy to hide small fraudulent charges within a bill; even if such a charge is detected, it is questionable whether the user would pursue a refund or the operator would investigate in any great depth.

  As a further impediment to detection of such malfeasance, users are generally conditioned to trust the phone infrastructure based on their experience with PSTN; while these perceptions remain and are transferred over to VoIP systems, they present a level of vulnerability at the human level. Thus, large-scale compromise and exploitation of accounts at low levels, potentially resulting in large aggregate sums, are feasible and relatively hard to detect. Other types of misbehavior (e.g., Caller ID spoofing) are also much easier with some VoIP infrastructures than is generally the case with PSTN because of this misplaced trust.

- *Use of common carrier:* VoIP and data traffic are often handled by the same networking infrastructure — indeed, this is one of the cost- and complexity-reduction benefits that VoIP systems promise. However, this elimination of carrier diversity brings its own risks. One problem is that attacks on one component can usually easily spill over, affecting the other: consider, for example, network denial of service attacks or compromise of the VoIP billing system by breaking into the administrator's email account. A second problem is that a sufficiently advanced adversary can then control two means of communication with the outside world that are generally thought of as independent. As a result, certain common actions we might take today because of trusting in the carrier independence principle become much riskier. Consider, for example, a phishing email claiming there is a problem with the user's bank account; however, rather than inviting the user to go to the bank's web site, the advice is to call the number on the back of the card. Although we might consider this as a good way to authenticate the callee (the bank's customer service number), this would not be the case if the local VoIP gateway or end-user device was compromised and programmed to redirect calls.

- *Real-time aspect:* Finally, the real-time element of voice and video content carried by VoIP placed severe latency limitations on any defensive measures. As a comparative example, ISPs can often delay email delivery by several minutes, in order to better determine if it is spam. Similar action for VoIP calls is not viewed as feasible.

In trying to understand the threat space against VoIP, our approach is to place known vulnerabilities within a structured framework. While a single taxonomy is not likely to be definitive, using several different viewpoints and mapping the vulnerability space along several axis may reveal trends and areas that merit further analysis.

As a starting point, we use the taxonomy provided by the Voice over IP Security Alliance (VoIPSA)[1]. VoIPSA is a vendor-neutral, not for profit organization com-

---

[1] http://www.voipsa.org/

posed of VoIP and security vendors, organizations and individuals with an interest in securing VoIP protocols, products and installations. In addition, we place the surveyed vulnerabilities within the traditional threat space of confidentiality, integrity, availability (CIA). Finally, we consider whether the vulnerabilities exploit bugs in the protocol, implementation or system configuration. In future work, we hope to expand the number of views to the surveyed vulnerabilities and to provide more in-depth analysis. We will not be discussing in detail the specific means for exercising these vulnerabilities; the interested reader is referred to the already available literature [71].

The VoIPSA security threat taxonomy[264] aims to define the security threats against VoIP deployments, services, and end users. The key elements of this taxonomy are:

1. **Social threats** are aimed directly against humans. For example, misconfigurations, bugs or bad protocol interactions in VoIP systems may enable or facilitate attacks that misrepresent the identity of malicious parties to users. Such attacks may then act as stepping stones to further attacks such as phishing, theft of service, or unwanted contact (spam).
2. **Eavesdropping, interception, and modification threats** cover situations where an adversary can unlawfully and without authorization from the parties concerned listen in on the signaling (call setup) or the content of a VoIP session, and possibly modify aspects of that session while avoiding detection. Examples of such attacks include call re-routing and interception of unencrypted RTP sessions.
3. **Denial of service threats** have the potential to deny users access to VoIP services. This may be particularly problematic in the case of emergencies, or when a DoS attack affects all of a user's or organization's communication capabilities (i.e., when all VoIP and data communications are multiplexed over the same network which can be targeted through a DoS attack). Such attacks may be VoIP-specific (exploiting flaws in the call setup or the implementation of services), or VoIP-agnostic (e.g., generic traffic flooding attacks). They may also involve attacks with physical components (e.g., physically disconnecting or severing a cable) or through computing or other infrastructures (e.g., disabling the DNS server, or shutting down power).
4. **Service abuse threats** covers the improper use of VoIP services, especially (but not exclusively) in those situations where such services are offered in a commercial setting. Examples of such threats include toll fraud and billing avoidance [255, 256].
5. **Physical access threats** refer to inappropriate/unauthorized physical access to VoIP equipment, or to the physical layer of the network (following the ISO 7-layer network stack model).
6. **Interruption of services threats** refer to non-intentional problems that may nonetheless cause VoIP services to become unusable or inaccessible. Examples of such threats include loss of power due to inclement weather, resource exhaustion due to over-subscription, and performance issues that degrade call quality.

In our discussion of vulnerabilities (whether theoretical or demonstrated) that follows, we shall mark each item with a tuple (V, T, K), where:

- $V \in \{1, 2, 3, 4, 5, 6\}$, where each number refers to an element in the VoIPSA threat taxonomy from above
- $T \in \{C_1, I_1, A_1\}$, referring to Confidentiality, Integrity and Availability respectively
- $K \in \{P_2, I_2, C_2\}$, referring to Protocol, Implementation and Configuration respectively

For example, an item marked as $(1, C_1, C_2)$ refers to a vulnerability that targets the user (Social threat), violating Confidentiality via a Configuration problem or bug. In some cases, the same underlying vulnerability may be used to perform different types of attacks. We will be discussing all such significant attack variants, and cite some CVE vulnerabilities as token examples where necessary.

3.1 Survey of Disclosed Vulnerabilities

Threats against VoIP system availability by exploiting implementation weaknesses are fairly common. For example, some implementations where shown to be vulnerable to crashes or hanging (livelock) when given empty, malformed, or large volumes of INVITE or other messages $(3, A_1, I_2)$. It is worth noting that the same vulnerability may be present across similar protocols on the same platform and product (CVE-2007-4291) due to code sharing and internal software structure, or to systems that need to understand VoIP protocols but are not nominally part of a VoIP system (CVE-2005-4464). The reason for the disproportionately large number of denial of service vulnerabilities is because of the ease with which such failure can be diagnosed, especially when the bug is discovered through automated testing tools (e.g., fuzzers). Many of these vulnerabilities may in fact be more serious than a simple denial of service due to a crash, and could possibly lead to remote code injection and execution.

Unexpected interactions between different technologies used in VoIP systems can also lead to vulnerabilities. For example, in some cases cross-site scripting (XSS) attacks were demonstrated against the administrator- and customer-facing management interface (which was web-based) by injecting malicious Javascript in selected SIP messages $(1, I_1, I_2)$, often through SQL injection vulnerabilities (CVE-2008-6509). The same vulnerability could also be used to commit toll fraud by targeting the underlying database $(4, I_1, I_2)$. XSS attacks that are not web-oriented have also been demonstrated, with one of the oldest VoIP-related vulnerabilities (CVE-1999-0938) permitting shell command execution $(1, I_1, I_2)$. Another web-oriented attack vector is Cross Site Request Forgery (CSRF), whereby users visiting a malicious page can be induced to automatically (without user intervention, and often without any observable indications) perform some action on the web servers (in this case, VoIP web-based management interface) that their browser is already authenticated to (CVE-2008-1250) $(1,I_1,I_2)$. Other privilege-escalation vulnerabilities through the web interface also exist (CVE-2008-6708) $(1,I_1,I_2)$.

The complexity of the SIP finite state machine has sometimes led to poor implementations. For example, one vulnerability (CVE-2007-4498) allowed attackers to confuse a phone receiving a call into silently completing the call, which allowed the adversary to eavesdrop on the device's surroundings $(2,C_1,I_2)$. The same vulnerability could be used to deny call reception at the target, since the device was already marked as busy $(3,A_1,I_2)$. In other cases, it is unclear to developers what use of a specific protocol field may be, in which case they may silently ignore it. Occasionally, such information is critical for the security of the protocol exchange, and omitting or not checking it allows adversaries to perform attacks such as man-in-the-middle or traffic interception (CVE-2007-3319) $(2,C_1+I_1,I_2)$, or to bypass authentication checks (CVE-2007-3177) $(4,I_1,I_2)$.

Since SIP devices are primarily software-driven, they are vulnerable to the same classes of vulnerabilities as other software. For example, buffer overflows are possible even against SIP "hardphones", much less softphones, allowing adversaries to gain complete control of the device $(2,I_1,I_2)$. Such vulnerabilities typically arise from a combination of poor (non-defensive) programming practices, insufficient testing, and the use of languages, such as C and C++ that support unsafe operations. Sometimes, these vulnerabilities appear in software that is not directly used in VoIP but must be VoIP-aware, e.g., firewalls (CVE-2003-0819) or protocol analyzers (CVE-2005-1461) $(2,I_1,I_2)$. It is also worth noting that these are not the only types of vulnerabilities that can lead to remote code execution. Other input validation failures can allow attackers to download arbitrary files from a user's machine $(1,C_1,I_2)$ or to place calls (CVE-2008-1334) $(1,I_1,I_2)$ by supplying specially encoded URIs (CVE-2006-2312) or other parameters.

A significant risk with VoIP devices is the ability of adversaries to misrepresent their identity (e.g., their calling number). Such vulnerabilities (CVE-2005-2181) sometimes arise due to the lack of cross-checking of information provided across several messages during call setup and throughout the session $(1,I_1,I_2)$.

Similar failures to cross-check and validate information can lead to other attacks, such as indicating whether there is pending voicemail for the user (CVE-2005-2182) $(1,I_1,I_2)$, or where attackers may spoof incoming calls by directly connecting to a VoIP phone (CVE-2007-5791) $(1,I_1,I_2)$.

Undocumented, on-by-default features are another source of vulnerabilities. These are often remnants from testing and debugging during development that were not disabled when a product shipped (CVE-2006-0305). As a result, they often offer privileged access to services and data on a device that would not be otherwise available $(1,C_1,I_2)$. One particularly interesting vulnerability allowed an attacker to place outgoing calls through the web management interface (CVE-2008-1248) $(4,I_1,C_2)$.

A significant class of vulnerabilities in VoIP devices revolves around default configurations, and in particular default usernames and passwords $(2,C_1+I_1,C_2)$. Lists of default accounts are easy to find on the Internet via a search engine. Users often do not change these settings; ironically, this seems to be particularly so for administrative accounts, which are rarely (if ever) used in the home/SOHO environment. Other default settings involve NTP servers (CVE-2006-0375) and DNS servers (CVE-2005-3725) $(2, C_1 + I_1, C_2)$.

Call interception vulnerabilities are a big concern with VoIP systems, given the plethora of tools for decoding video and audio streams and the ease of eavesdropping network traffic, especially on the local subnet. Sometimes, such vulnerabilities arise from strange protocol interactions and implementation decisions. For example, caching the location (address) of a VoIP phone based on the IP address used during boot time (using TFTP) seems a reasonable approach; however, since the boot and VoIP stacks are not necessarily tightly integrated, interaction with one protocol can have adverse effects (e.g., changing the perceived location of the phone) in the other protocol (CVE-2007-5361) $(2, C_1, I_2)$. Other instances of such vulnerabilities involve improper/insufficient credential checking by the registrar or proxy (CVE-2008-5871) or by the SNMP server (CVE-2005-3722), which can lead to traffic interception $(2, C_1, I_2)$ and user impersonation $(1, I_1, I_2)$.

The integration of several capabilities in VoIP products, e.g., a web server used for the management interface, can lead to vulnerabilities being imported to the VoIP environment that would not otherwise apply. In the specific example of an integrated web server, directory traversal bugs (CVE-2008-4875) or similar problems (such as lack of proper authentication in the web interface) (CVE-2008-6707) can allow adversaries to read arbitrary files or other information from the device $(1, C_1, I_2)$. SIP (or, more generally, VoIP) components integrated with firewalls may also interact in undesirable ways. For example, improper handling of registration requests may allow attackers to receive messages intended for other users (CVE-2007-6095) $(2, C_1, I_2)$. Other such examples include failure to authenticate server certificates in wireless environments, enabling man-in-the-middle and eavesdropping attacks (CVE-2008-1114) $(2, C_1, I_2)$.

Predictability and lack of proper use (or sources) of randomness is another vulnerability seen in VoIP products. For example, predictable values in SIP header messages (CVE-2002-1935) allows malicious users to avoid registering but continue using the service $(4, I_1, I_2)$.

Protocol responses to carefully crafted messages can reveal information about the system or its users to an attacker. Although this has been long understood in limited-domain protocols (e.g., remote login), with measures taken to normalize responses such that no information is leaked, the complexity of VoIP (and other) protocols make this infeasible. As a result, information disclosure vulnerabilities abound (CVE-2008-3903) $(1, C_1, I_2)$.

Some of the most serious non-implementation type of vulnerabilities are those where the specification permits behavior that is exploitable. For example, certain vendors permit the actual URI in a SIP INVITE call and the URI used as part of the Digest Authentication to differ, which (while arguably permitted by the specification) allows credential reuse and toll fraud (CVE-2007-5469) $(4, I_1, P_2)$.

While rare, protocol-level vulnerabilities also exist. These represent either outright bugs in the specification, or unforeseen interaction between different protocols

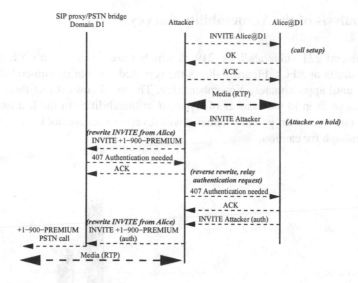

Fig. 6 SIP relay attack

or protocol components. For large, complicated protocols such as SIP and H.323, where components (code, messages, etc.) are semantically overloaded and reused, it is perhaps not surprising that such emergent properties exist. One good example is the relay attack possible with the SIP Digest Authentication [249], whereby an adversary can reuse another party's credentials to obtain unauthorized access to SIP or PSTN services (such as calling a premium or international phone line) $(4, I_1, P_2)$. This attack, depicted in Fig. 6, is possible because authentication may be requested in response to an INVITE message at any time during a call, and the responder may issue an INVITE message during a call either automatically (because of timer expirations) or through a user action (e.g., placing the caller on hold in order to do a call transfer).

Another protocol-level vulnerability, discovered 6 years after the original SIP RFC was published, involves the abuse of call forwarding and splitting (e.g., for conference calls or multi-presence) to amplify a small number of SIP requests into a much larger number of inter-proxy messages and traffic [243]. It is worthwhile noting that packet amplifications problems have been identified over the years in a number of networking protocols, including IP (hence the use of a Time-To-Live field) and SIP itself. However, in the case of SIP, the settings specified by RFC 3261 turned out to be both insufficient and too lenient.

3.2 Analysis of the Vulnerability Survey

We examined 221 vulnerabilities, 219 of which were disclosed in CVE and 2 as Internet drafts or RFCs. Figure 7 shows the reported number of vulnerabilities per year, up until approximately November 2009. The good news is that there appears to be a large drop in the number of *reported* vulnerabilities in the last two years. The reasons for this drop (and whether it will revert or not) are not known, which is reason enough for caution.

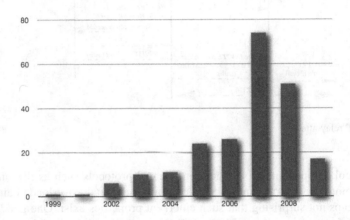

Fig. 7 Vulnerability distribution over time

Looking at the vulnerabilities we have considered, a few patterns emerge. First, as we can see in our informal classification of vulnerability effects show in Fig. 8, half of the problems lead to a denial of service in either an end-device (phone, soft-phone) or a server (proxy, registrar, etc.). This is not altogether surprising, since denial of service (especially a crash) is something that is easily diagnosed. In many cases, the problem was discovered by automated testing, such as protocol or software fuzzing; software failures are relatively easy to determine in such settings. Some of these vulnerabilities could in fact turn out to be more serious, e.g., a memory corruption leading to a crash could be exploitable to mount a code injection attack. The second largest class of vulnerabilities allows an adversary to control the device, whether by code injection, default passwords and services, or authentication failures. Note that we counted a few of the vulnerabilities (approximately 10%) more than once in this classification.

The same pattern with respect to the predominance of denial of service vulnerabilities holds when we look at the breakdown according to the VoIPSA taxonomy, shown in Fig. 9. Figure 10 shows the distribution of vulnerabilities across multiple categories (since a given vulnerability could lead in different types of compromise). It should not be surprising that, given the nature of the vulnerabilities disclosed in CVE, we have no data on physical access and (accidental) interruption of services

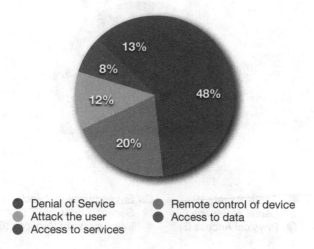

Fig. 8 Vulnerability breakdown based on effect. Most categories are self-explanatory; "attack the user" refers to vulnerabilities that permit attackers to affect the user/administrator of a device, without necessarily compromising the system or getting access to its data or services. XSS attacks and traffic eavesdropping attacks fall in this category, whereas attacks that compromise state (data) resident on the system fall in the "access to data" category.

vulnerabilities. Furthermore, while "Access to Services" was a non-negligible component in the previous breakdown, it represents only 4% here. The reason for this apparent discrepancy is in the different definitions of service: the specific element in the VoIPSA taxonomy refers to VoIP-specific abuse, whereas our informal definition covers lower-level system components which may not be usable in, for example, placing fraudulent calls. One other observation here is that, while the VoIPSA taxonomy covers a broad spectrum of concerns for VoIP system designers and operators, its categories are too perhaps too broad (and, in some cases, imprecise) to help with characterizing the types of bugs we have examined.

The vulnerability breakdown according to the traditional (Confidentiality, Integrity, Availability) security concerns again reflects the predominance of denial of service threats against VoIP systems, as seen in Fig. 11. However, we can see that Integrity violations (e.g., system compromise) are a sizable component of the threat space, while Confidentiality violations are seen in only 15% of disclosed vulnerabilities. This represents an inversion of the perceived threats by users and administrators, who (anecdotal evidence suggests) typically worry about such issues as call interception and eavesdropping. Figure 12 shows the distribution of vulnerabilities across multiple bins (where each vulnerability may contribute to multiple violation types).

Figure 13 shows the breakdown based on source of vulnerability. The overwhelming majority of reported problems arise from implementation issues, which should not be surprising given the nature of bug disclosure. Problems arising from

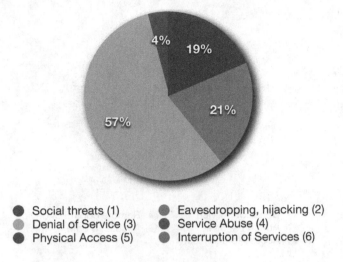

Social threats (1)   Eavesdropping, hijacking (2)
Denial of Service (3)   Service Abuse (4)
Physical Access (5)   Interruption of Services (6)

Fig. 9 Vulnerability breakdown based on VoIPSA taxonomy

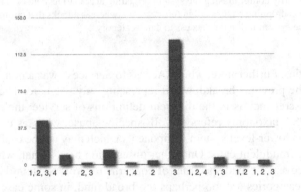

Fig. 10 VoIPSA taxonomy with multiple-bin assignment

configuration represented 7% of the total space, including such items as privileged services left on and default username/passwords. However, note that the true picture (i.e., what actually happens with deployed systems) is probably different in that configuration problems are most likely undercounted: such problems are often site-specific and are not reported to bug-disclosure databases when discovered. On the other hand, implementation and protocol problems are prime candidates for disclosure. What is surprising is the presence of protocol vulnerabilities; one would expect that such problems were discovered and issued during protocol development,

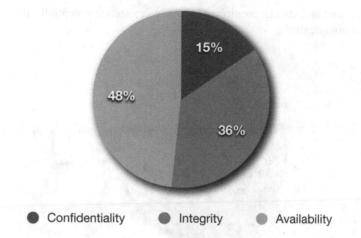

Fig. 11 Vulnerability breakdown based on "traditional" security classification (C_1, I_1, A_1)

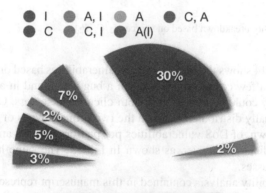

Fig. 12 Multiple-bin vulnerability classification using "traditional" violations

specification, and standardization. Their mere existence potentially indicates high
protocol complexity.

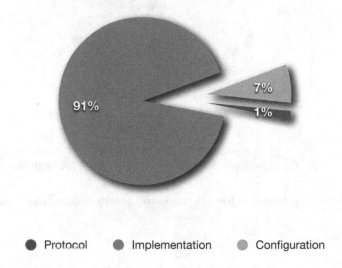

Fig. 13 Vulnerability breakdown based on source (I_2, C_2, P_2)

Finally, Fig. 14 shows the breakdown of vulnerabilities based on the affected type
of platform. In a few cases, typically when a bug was found in a software library,
the vulnerability could be exploited in both clients and servers. Otherwise, vulnerabilities are equally distributed between the two primary types of VoIP platform. A
similar breakdown, of DoS vulnerabilities per platform, shows an even more equal
split between client and server, as shown in Fig 15. The same holds of the other
vulnerability classes.

The vulnerability analysis contained in this manuscript represents, by its nature,
a static snapshot: we have presented a view of known problems with VoIP systems, with no correlation with (and knowledge of) actual attacks exploiting these,
or other vulnerabilities. A complete analysis of the threat space would also contain
a dynamic component, whereby attacker behavior patterns and trends would be analyzed vis-a-vis actual, deployed VoIP systems or, lacking access to such, simulacra
thereof [175].

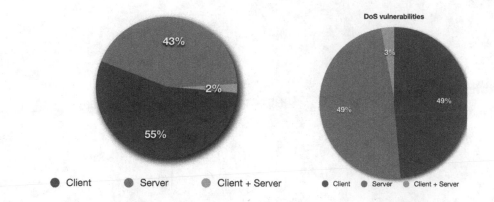

Fig. 14 Vulnerabilities per platform   **Fig. 15** DoS vulnerabilities per platform

4
Survey of VoIP Security Research Literature

4.1 Collection Methodology

We followed a structured approach to compiling the list of papers. While we do not claim to have all VoIP security papers, we have identified as many as was possible using our methodology. The process we used was:

- Compile an initial collection of papers, based on:

  - Personal knowledge (direct and through recommendation) of specific papers.
  - Searches on CiteSeer, IEEE Xplore, ACM Digital Library and Google Scholar (keywords used were "VoIP security", "SIP security", "VoIP vulnerabilities", "SIP vulnerabilities", "SIP attacks", "VoIP attacks").
  - Browsing the proceedings of top security conferences and journals (IEEE Security & Privacy Symposium, ISOC Symposium on Network and Distributed Systems Security, ACM Computer and Communications Security, USENIX Security, RAID, ACM Transactions on Information and Systems Security, IEEE Transactions on Dependable and Secure Computing), and some area-specific workshops (e.g., VoIP Security Workshop) from the past 5 years.

- Expand this selection by:

  - Fetching all relevant cited papers not already in the collection.
  - Browsing the proceedings of conferences or journals in which these cited papers appeared, to identify other relevant papers.
  - Searching for other VoIP security papers by the authors of these cited papers.

- Iterate until no new papers are added to the collection.

Amusingly, in the process of compiling and processing this body of work, we identified one case of plagiarism between papers by different authors that were published 6 years apart.

In order to avoid a lopsided distribution of papers (and an infinite expansion), we did not include in the collection papers that were deemed of only peripheral relevance to VoIP or VoIP security. The result of this process (modulo any papers inadvertently missed) was 245 publications.

4.2 Extended VoIPSA Classification

In our discussion and classification of related work that follows, we focus on the first four elements of the VoIPSA taxonomy that we discussed in Sec. 3, since the last two are largely outside the scope of computer security research. In addition to these four categories, we also use the following:

- **Overviews and Surveys** covers work that does not offer any original technical research, but rather summarize attacks and defenses in VoIP. While valuable in helping understand the problem space, such works are generally (but not always) fairly narrow in scope and do not typically suggest solutions to the problems surveyed; at best, they summarize existing/known techniques and mechanisms for mitigating those problems.
- **Field Studies and System/Protocol Analysis** covers work that analyzes software, protocols, and systems using a variety of techniques.
- **Performance Analysis** covers work that measures the performance impact of security mechanisms, both on call setup (authentication costs) and on media transfer.
- **Authentication Protocols** covers work that proposes extensions or variants of authentication mechanisms and algorithms with SIP. Typically, these papers have a strong cryptographic element, with VoIP used primarily as a motivating environment.
- **Architectures** covers work that defines cross-cutting approaches to secure VoIP. In the surveyed work, a significant portion of these papers revolves around intrusion detection systems.
- **Middleboxes** covers work that describes new firewall architectures or mechanisms for enabling VoIP to work with the current generation of firewalls.
- **Intrusion Detection** covers other intrusion and anomaly detection work that could not be easily classified in any of the previous categories.
- **Miscellaneous** includes other work that does not fit in the remainder of the classification.

Figure 16 graphically depicts our overall classification scheme, annotated with the number of items in each category.

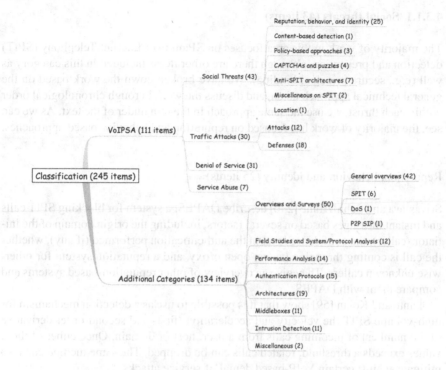

Fig. 16 Classification tree for surveyed research literature

4.3 Survey of VoIP Security Research

In the following two sections, we discuss the related work using the extended VoIPSA taxonomy, as described in Subsec. 4.2. For each classification area, we give the paper count as a crude indication of the level of activity.

4.3.1 VoIPSA-based Classification (111 items)

We now discuss the work that fits naturally within the first four categories of the VoIPSA taxonomy, which constitutes 45% of the surveyed papers. All other work is further classified and discussed in Sec. 4.3.2.

4.3.1.1 Social threats (43 items)

The majority of work in this area focuses on SPam over Internet Telephony (SPIT) detection and prevention, although there are other items included in this category as well (e.g., secure principal binding). We have broken down the work based on the general technical approach taken, and discuss the work in rough chronological order within each thrust; we use the same approach in the remainder of the text. As we can see, the majority of work has focused on reputation and behavior-based approaches.

Reputation, behavior, and identity (25 items)

Srivastava and Schulzrinne [246] describe DAPES, a system for blocking SPIT calls and instant messages based on several factors, including the origin domain of the initiator (caller), the confidence level in the authentication performed (if any), whether the call is coming through a known open proxy, and a reputation system for otherwise unknown callers. They give an overview of other reputation-based systems and compare them with DAPES.

Dantu and Kolan [59] show that it is possible to use as a detection mechanism for high-volume SPIT the velocity and acceleration (first- and second-order derivative of the number) of incoming calls from a user, host or domain. Once either of these values exceeds a threshold, related calls can be dropped. The same method can also mitigate against certain VoIP-based denial of service attacks.

MacIntosh and Vinokurov [154] propose a statistical detection algorithm for SPIT that can be implemented at the receiver's server. For each external entity that communicates with local users, their system keeps track of the number of call setups and terminations in both directions (incoming and outgoing). Simultaneous deviation of two or more of these counters from their assumed long-term averages supposedly indicates spam activity, with confidence increasing as the deviation widens. The approach assumes that attackers cannot rapidly change their identity.

Croft and Olivier [55] propose extending the call setup process by adding a "call me back" scheme using a Verifying Authority (VA) and a Mediator. The Mediator acts as a call bridge, allowing the call to connect only once the VA has approved it (possibly based on policy and on such information as caller/callee identities, location and time of the call, etc.). The user receives the "call me back" request from the VA, and decides whether to proceed with picking up the call based on local policy and other information (e.g., CallerID).

Dantu and Kolan [60, 139] describe the Voice Spam Detector (VSD), a multi-stage SPIT filter based on trust, reputation, and feedback among the various filter stages. The primary filter stages are call pattern and volume analysis, black and white lists of callers, per-caller behavior profile based on Bayesian classification and prior history, and reputation information from the callee's contacts and social network. They provide a formal model for trust and reputation in a voice network, based on intuitive human behavior. They evaluate their system in a laboratory experiment using a small number of real users and injected SPIT calls.

Rebahi and Sisalem [199] develop the concept of the "SIP social network" as a means for managing reputation toward countering SPIT. However, no experimental evaluation or validation of any of these schemes is performed. Rebahi et al. [200] extend the previous by proposing two schemes for protecting against SPIT and SPIM (spam over instant messaging). The first uses reputation, with users indicating how much "trust" they have in the persons in their contact lists. These lists (and the trust values) are posted in a directory, where others can access them upon receiving a call from a previously unknown (to them) entity. This scheme requires that every user's contact information be published, and that attackers cannot mask or change their identities. The second scheme is built around the notion of "payment at risk", wherein a caller may be required to deposit a small amount to a SIP server prior to placing a call, depending on the callee's or the SIP proxy's policy. If the user indicates that the call was SPIT, the payment is then forfeit.

Hansen et al. [115] present SPIT-AL, an anomaly detection system seeking to identify SPIT calls. Their system takes into consideration information about the caller (such as CallerID, IP address, whitelists/blacklists, etc.) and the call (e.g., time), and allows for different responses (grey-listing, audio CAPTCHA, etc.). A key element of their architecture is that users manage their own rules and responses, in order to comply with the various German telecommunication laws.

Baumann et al. [29] overview SPIT threats and various defense mechanisms. They then propose to prevent Sybil attacks in SIP by binding user identities to biometric information (specifically voice fingerprint) that is stored in global servers. Users wishing to place calls must first prove their identity, thereafter receiving credentials that can be used to place calls.

Madhosingh [155] integrates white and black lists with CAPTCHAs for those callers that are not known a priori (and included in a whitelist or a blacklist). If the test is passed, the call is allowed through. However, such callers are not allowed to leave voicemail messages to the callee's system; instead, such messages are stored on the caller's local SIP server, and the callee is sent an indication about the availability of a voicemail and instructions on how to retrieve it.

Bertrand et al. [33] propose an anomaly detection technique for identifying and blocking SPIT that creates caller profiles based on their IP address. The criteria used by in their analysis includes number of received error messages, the use of a directory service, whether multiple calls are placed by the same caller, the duration of calls and the variance of call duration across multiple calls, and the number of simultaneous incoming calls (from multiple different users) to the same user. In response to an identified SPIT call, their system rate limits call delivery, temporary blacklists the most aggressive callers, or redirects the call to a voicemail or other automated system that notifies the caller of the problem. They propose implementing this functionality in the network, where it will work together with routers. Because of this choice, their system must do real-time layer 7 reconstruction and analysis of traffic, which in turn requires hardware support to keep up with the volume. Such a system should be able to handle up to 10^6 simultaneous sessions, for 10^5 subscribers, with 10^4 incoming calls per second. They present a prototype Java-based implementation running on Linux, using the `netfilter` and `iptables` components to divert and block traffic. Their performance evaluation shows that this prototype can handle 80 incoming calls per second, adding approximately 5ms to the average 5.8 seconds call establishment time.

Yan et al. [281] argue for the use of active fingerprinting in SPIT prevention systems. Protocol implementations interpret the standards in slightly different ways, especially with respect to indicating errors. Thus, it is possible to identify the implementation of a peer SIP device by observing its responses to a set of specially crafted messages. These may be either standards-compliant or non-compliant. By creating a number of different tests, it is possible to actively fingerprint a remote SIP device that is trying to initiate a call. Their conjecture is that malicious SIP user agents will not be able to mimic legitimate stacks because of the diversity in possible responses, and because often such tools implement only a subset of SIP. In their analysis, they were able to create unique fingerprints for 20 different SIP devices. The system evaluation was limited to a performance (throughput) oriented experiment using PlanetLab.

Balasubramaniyan et al. [22] propose to use call duration and social network graphs to establish a measure of reputation for callers. Their intuition is that users whose call graph has a relatively small fan-out and whose call durations are relatively long are less likely to be spammers. Conversely, users who place a lot of very short calls are likely to be engaging in SPIT. Furthermore, spammers will receive few (if any) calls. Their system works both when the parties in a call have a social network link between them, and when such a link does not exist by assigning global reputation scores. Users that are mistakenly categorized as spammers are redirected to a Turing test, allowing them to complete the call if they answer correctly. In a simulation-based evaluation, the authors determine that their system can achieve a false negative rate of 10% and a false positive rate of 3%, even in the presence of large numbers of spammers.

Ono and Schulzrinne [180] propose the use of weak social ties as a means to label calls with unknown or incomplete caller ID information, in conjunction with a blacklist/whitelist filtering scheme. As one specific mechanism, they describe the use of weakly secret information that a user makes available to potential callers, who must then use that information in future calls. Another similar technique involves callers providing contact/identifying information to potential future callees. Both of these schemes exploit cross-media interactions, leveraging the fact that most calls are associated with some other interaction between the caller and callee entities. For example, an e-commerce web site may accept such a weak secret from a customer, or provide one (depending on the scheme); this secret would then be used when calling the customer in the future.

Guang-Yu et al. [106] describe a multi-layer SPIT detection and prevention architecture that takes into consideration the behavioral characteristics of specific types of SPIT campaigns, starting from the reconnaissance phase.

Patankar et al. [183] compare two SPIT detectors derived from the email spam domain. One of these techniques is based on user reputation through a referral social network model, while the other assigns a trust value to incoming SIP messages based on their direct prior interactions with the caller. Their simulations indicate that the referral-based model is more effective, correctly identifying SPIT in over 98% of cases. In an environment with little-to-moderate amounts of SPI, this likely be sufficient by itself. If the level of SPIT approaches the current (circa 2010) levels of email spam, then additional filtering/blocking mechanisms would have to be employed.

Wu et al. [277] apply semi-supervised clustering to call parameters (with optional user feedback) in order to distinguish SPIT from non-SPIT calls. The evaluation, which was done using manually created call traces, shows that the approach is scalable (in the number of calls) and offers reasonable detection performance. Hyung-Jong et al. [127] describe a behavior-based system that seeks to identify likely SPIT callers.

Sorge and Seedorf [241] apply reputation techniques to the SPIT problem, by evaluating the quality of information (tags) attached to outgoing calls by the callers' SIP-based service provider (SSP). Their scheme allows receiving SIP providers to evaluate the likelihood of a call being SPIT using caller-SSP information, providing incentives to honest SSPs to correctly tag their outbound calls. They demonstrate, through analytical means, that the precision of their SPIT detection improves by almost 50% even in a limited trust case, with greater improvements as longer trust chains of SSPs are taken into consideration.

Phithakkitnukoon and Dantu propose the use of user feedback in closed email systems (such as Gmail) to identify spammers [186]. The challenge in their scheme, which envisions a binary "spammer/non-spammer" classification is to choose an appropriate threshold for determining when this transition occurs so as not to misclassify benign users who were accidentally or maliciously tagged as spammers.

Content-based detection (1 item)

Pörschmann and Knospe [187] propose a SPIT detection mechanism based on applying spectral analysis to the audio data of VoIP calls to create acoustic fingerprints. SPIT calls are identified by detecting a large number of fingerprints across a large number of different calls.

Policy-based approaches (3 items)

Tschofenig et al. [261] propose the use of a SIP Authentication service that uses the Security Assertion Markup Language (SAML) to specify authentication requirements for SIP callers prior to placing a call. The relevant information (e.g., identity) is then forwarded to the receiver, which can use similar SAML policies to determine whether they are willing to receive the call.

d'Heureuse et al. [63] describe an anti-SPIT system that integrates user roles and personal preferences in its approach to blocking unwanted calls. Their system allows users to express their requirements and current status using a policy language based on an extended version of the IETF-standardized Call Processing Language (CPL).

The authors give some paper examples of how users might use such a system, and briefly describe a prototype implementation.

Soupionis et al. [242] propose a policy-based approach for defending against SPIT. They use a rules-based approach to SPIT detection, combined with a number of mitigation strategies and mechanisms that policy can invoke in response to detection.

CAPTCHAs and puzzles (4 items)

Banerjee et al. [23] propose the use of computational puzzles as part of the identity (public/private key pair) generation phase in peer-to-peer VoIP networks to prevent spammers from creating large numbers of disposable identities. Once identities become harder to generate on demand, trust and reputation-based mechanisms can be used to manage SPIT.

Quittek et al. [193] propose the use of *hidden* Turing tests to identify SPIT callers. As a concrete approach, they leverage the interaction model in human conversation, which minimizes the amount of simultaneous ("double") talk by the participants, and the fact that there is a short pause at the beginning of an answered call, followed by a statement by the callee that initiates the conversation. By looking for signs of violation of such norms, it is possible to identify naïve automated SPIT callers. The authors implement their scheme and integrate it with a VoIP firewall.

Wang [269] describes an end-point audio CAPTCHA system for countering SPIT, meant to be installed and used by users and system administrators. She conducts a usability study, examining the installation and management overhead of the tool (including the design and recording of challenge questions), the understandability and time-to-answer of the system and the questions by legitimate callers, and correctness in answering. For the latter metric, she focuses specifically on English-as-Second-Language users. Lindqvist and Komu [130] describe a similar approach using image human-interaction proofs in conjunction with SIP.

Anti-SPIT architectures (7 items)

Niccolini [177] discusses the difficulties in protecting against IP telephony spam (SPIT) and overviews the various approaches for blocking such calls, identifying the technical and operational problems with each. Possible building blocks for SPIT prevention include blacklists/whitelists combined with strong identity verification to provide a reliable CallerID system, referral-based systems among trusted SIP domains [112, 214], pattern or anomaly detection techniques to discriminate SPIT based on training data, multi-level grey-listing of calls based on caller behavior (similar to throttling) [231, 232], computational puzzles and CAPTCHAs, explicit callee consent (a form of capability, required to actually place a call), content filtering on voicemail spam, callee feedback to indicate whether a call was SPIT or legitimate (typically combined with whitelisting/blacklisting, and requiring strong identity), changing one's SIP address as soon as SPIT messages arrive, requiring a monetary fee for the first contact, and legal action. Niccolini argues that none of these methods by itself is likely to succeed, promotes a modular and extensible approach to SPIT prevention, and presents a high-level architecture with these properties that was designed for use in a commercial SIP router.

Schlegel et al. [216] describe a framework for preventing SPIT. They argue for a modular approach to identifying SPIT, using hints from both signaling and media transfer. The first stage of their system looks at information that is available prior to accepting the call, while the second stage interacts with a caller (possibly prior to passing on the call to the callee). The various components integrated in their system include whitelists/blacklists, call statistics, IP/domain correlation, and Turing tests. Their system also allows for feedback from the callee to be integrated into the scoring mechanism, for use in screening future calls. The evaluation focuses on scalability, by measuring the response time to calls as call volumes increase. A similar architecture, with some additional components, is described by Quittek et al. [192] and later extended [194].

The SPIDER project (SPam over Internet telephony Detection sERvice) third public report [201] describes an anti-SPIT architectural framework. (The first two reports are described later, in Sec. 4.3.2.1.) Elements of this architecture include improved authentication, whitelisting/blacklisting, behavior analysis, the use of computational puzzles for challenge/response, reputation management, and audio content analysis.

Mathieu et al. [162] describe SDRS, an anti-SPIT system that combines several of detection schemes and takes into consideration users' and operators' preferences. Gritzalis and Mallios [105] survey various defenses against SPIT, and propose an integrated framework for mitigating the various limitations of each individual mechanism.

Miscellaneous on SPIT (2 items)

Kolan et al. [140] use traces of voice calls in a university environment to validate a mathematical model for computing the nuisance level of an incoming call, using feedback from the receivers. The model is intended to be used in predicting SPIT calls in VoIP environments, and is based on the history of prior communications between the two parties involved, which includes explicit feedback from the receiver indicating that a call is unwanted (at a particular point in time). Dritsas et al. [68] combine several criteria that they argue define a SPIT call with an ontology for SPIT, towards improving the management of SPIT incidents.

Location (1 item)

Kong et al. [141] propose a scheme for securing the user location information in SIP, i.e., the integrity and authenticity of the binding a principal's SIP URI and a correponding device's contact/network address. The threat addressed is tampering with the location information of a user such that calls to that user are redirected to a malicious party (impersonation) or are dropped (denial of service). In their approach, users create temporary public keys that are bound to their location and identity through the SIP registration process, possibly leveraging the existing SIP authentication mechanism used (or using some out-of-bound mechanism for securing the binding). Users then digitally sign their registration information, which the local registrar verifies before sending to the location server. To allow entities in other domains to verify the location information, the user public key can be conveyed through a secure channel at the domain level, e.g., by leveraging registrar public key certificates, or a pairwise shared secret key between two domains. This approach assumes benign and reliable registrar servers. To mitigate this weakness in the assumptions and to improve overall service reliability, the authors also propose the use of Byzantine Fault Tolerance techniques, adapting their protocols (public key binding & querying, and user registration) to a quorum environment. They conduct an experimental evaluation of their non-replicated scheme, showing that it can achieve the same performance as unsecured SIP and is 3–50 times faster than TLS-protected SIP.

4.3.1.2 Eavesdropping, Interception, and Modification (30 items)

Considerable work has been dedicated to protecting and attacking VoIP signaling and data traffic. We divide the work in two sub-categories, attacks and defenses.

Attacks (12 items)

Wang et al. [52, 280] describe a de-anonymization attack against VoIP streams that use low-latency anonymity proxies. Their intuition is to insert a watermark in the encrypted stream, tracking its propagation across the network. The watermark used is a perturbation of the inter-packet delay for selected packets in the stream. With appropriate use of redundancy, they demonstrate a tracking attack against 2-minute Skype calls across the Internet using $3ms$ delays. Depending on the watermark parameters chosen, they can achieve 99% true positive and 0% false positive rate or 100% true positive and 0.1% false positive rate. Srivatsa et al. [248] demonstrate flow-analysis attacks that expose the privacy of peer-to-peer VoIP participants.

Shah et al. [228] examine the use of injected jitter into VoIP as a covert channel to exfiltrate keyboard activity of interest (e.g., passwords). This attack would be effective even when the VoIP stream is encrypted.

Takahashi and Lee [252] examine the problem of covert channels in VoIP protocols, identifying and quantifying several ways in which data can be surreptitiously leaked out of a user's system or an enterprise network. As an example, they demonstrate the steganographic insertion of a second voice channel in a SIP-based VoIP conversation. This has the potential of leaking an otherwise secure (encrypted) conversation through a secondary channel, or can be used to hide the true communication content from an eavesdropper. They determine such parameters as channel capacity and perceptual quality of the encoded signal through experimental evaluation. They conclude with a discussion of several possible countermeasures and detection methods.

Weiser et al. [272] provide an overview of the security considerations in RTP, the media transfer protocol used in both SIP and H.323. They analyze six different implementations, discovering confidentiality (eavesdropping a call), integrity (injecting voice into an ongoing call) and availability (performing DoS) compromises. This work assumes that no security mechanism (such as SRTP) is used.

Wright et al. [273] apply machine learning techniques to determine the language spoken in a VoIP conversation, when a variable bit rate (VBR) voice codec is used based on the length of the encrypted voice frame. As a countermeasure, they propose the use of block ciphers for encrypting the voice. In follow-on work [274] they use profile Hidden Markov Models to identify specific phrases in the encrypted voice stream with a 50% average accuracy, rising to 90% for certain phrases.

Wang et al. [270] evaluate the resilience of three commercial VoIP services (AT&T, Vonage and Gizmo) against man-in-the-middle adversaries. They show that it is possible for an attacker to divert and redirect calls in the first two services by modifying the RTP endpoint information included in the SDP exchange (which is not protected by the SIP Digest Authentication), and to manipulate a user's call forwarding settings in the latter two systems. These vulnerabilities permit for large-scale voice pharming, where unsuspecting users are directed to fake interactive voice response systems or human representatives. The authors argue for the need for TLS or IPsec protection of the signaling.

Verscheure et al. [263] exploit the nature of human conversation (i.e., alternating periods of talking and silence for each participant) to reveal communication pairs over a period of time. The technique does not work as well against systems that do not use silence suppression, as these effectively introduce a form of constant (voice) traffic padding in both directions.

Petraschek et al. [185] examine the usability and security of ZRTP, a key agreement protocol based on the Diffie Hellman key exchange, designed for use in VoIP environments that lack pre-established secret keys among users or a public key infrastructure (PKI). ZRTP is intended to be used with SRTP, which performs the actual content encryption and transfer. Because of the lack of a solid basis for authentication, which makes active man-in-the-middle attacks easy to launch, ZRTP uses Short Authentication Strings (SAS) to allow two users to verbally confirm that they have established the same secret key. The verbal communication serves as a weak form of authentication at the human level. The authors identify a relay attack in ZRTP, wherein a man-in-the-middle adversary can influence the SAS read by two legitimate users with whom he has established independent calls and ZRTP exchanges. The attacker can use one of the legitimate users as an oracle to pronounce the desired SAS string through a number of means, including social engineering. The authors point out that SAS does not offer any security in some communication scenarios with high security requirements, e.g., a user calling (or being called by) their bank. The authors implement their attack and demonstrate it in a lab environment.

Zhang et al. [290] show that, by exploiting DNS and VoIP implementation vulnerabilities, it is possible for attackers to perform man-in-the-middle attacks even when they are not on the direct communication path of the parties involved. They demonstrate their attack against Vonage, requiring that the attacker only knows the phone number and the IP address of the target phone. Such attacks can be used to eavesdrop and hijack the victims' VoIP calls. The authors recommend that users and operators use signaling and media protection, conduct fuzzing and testing of VoIP implementations, and develop a lightweight VoIP intrusion detection system to be deployed on the VoIP phone.

Defenses (18 items)

Guo et al. [107] propose a new scheme for protecting voice content that provides strong confidentiality guarantees while allowing for graceful voice degradation in the presence of packet loss. They evaluate their scheme via simulation and micro-benchmarks. However, Li et al. [152] show that the scheme is insecure.

Bellovin et al. [30] argue against the enactment of legislation (in the US) mandating the integration of lawful-intercept capabilities into VoIP implementations. Their key concerns is that, based on a history of system compromises and implementation weaknesses, mandating such capabilities would enable or ease attacks against personal communications by adversaries that would otherwise be unable to conduct such attacks. They suggest that lawful interception needs be met either at the application provider or the network link level.

Seedorf [221] proposes the use of cryptographically generated SIP URIs to protect the integrity of content in P2P SIP. Specifically, he uses self-certifying SIP URIs that encode a public key (or, more compactly, the hash of a public key). The owner of the corresponding private key can then post signed location binding information on the peer-to-peer network (e.g., Chord) that is used by call initiators to determine call routing.

Fessi et al. [83] propose extensions to P2P SIP that provide location and interaction privacy for participants. They develop a signaling protocol for P2P SIP that uses two different Kademlia-based overlay networks for storing information and forwarding traffic, respectively. Their scheme requires a centralized authentication server, which provides verifiable identities at the application/SIP layer. They consider attacks against their scheme, shared with more general anonymity systems (such as Tor). They use analytical models to estimate communication reliability, cryptographic overhead, and end-to-end signaling latency.

Talevski et al. [253] describe the addition of security (in the form of encryption and integrity protection) to a lightweight VoIP protocol suitable for mobile devices. Kuntze et al. [145] propose a mechanism for providing non-repudiation of voice content by using digital signatures, taking into consideration packet losses by reporting to the sender which packets were actually received.

Wang et al. [267] extend the SIP call setup to include a Diffie Hellman based key exchange that results in multiple shared keys that the parties switch among during the call in a deterministic (but unknown to an adversary) fashion. Their stated goal is to impede cryptanalytic attacks that depend on the same shared secret key being used throughout a call. They conduct a performance evaluation using a prototype implementation of their scheme on software phones, concluding that the overhead is negligible. The likely adoption of DTLS-SRTP would probably supersede this effort. Gurbani and Kolesnikov [109] discuss DTLS-SRTP and SDES (another proposed protocol for media protection), and propose a lightweight scheme that mitigates some of the performance concerns and security weaknesses of DTLS-SRTP.

Hlavacs et al. [121] propose the integration of computational puzzles in ZRTP as a way to mitigate the man-in-the-middle attack described earlier [185]. Effectively, their scheme places an upper bound to the amount of time a ZRTP exchange may take, placing the attacker under (hopefully) severe time constraint and making them unable to carry out the independent but parallel calls that are necessary. The authors propose a new puzzle scheme based on computing selected eigenvectors of real symmetric matrices. An additional protection mechanism suggested is to randomly delay (by short amounts of time) the receiving of calls, again trying to make more difficult the attacker's task of orchestrating and playing against each other two independent calls.

Palmieri and Fiore [182] describe an adaptation of SIP to provide end-to-end security using existing and well-known primitives (e.g., digital signatures and efficient encryption mechanisms). The authors developed a prototype implementation and conducted a performance analysis of their scheme. One drawback of this scheme relative to ZRTP is that it requires a PKI. When compared to at least some proposed deployments of DTLS-SRTP, this scheme provides end-to-end non-repudiation and end-to-end authentication while being resistant to man-in-the-middle attacks.

Zhang and Berthold [286] discuss several passive traffic analysis attacks on VoIP systems. These attacks exploit both signaling and media flow information. They also discuss techniques that can be used to mitigate some of these attacks, and conclude with a list of open problems. Many of the attacks and the countermeasures are shared with those in general-purpose anonymity systems. Zhang and Fischer-Hubner [287] and Melchor et al. [168] also discuss techniques for protecting the privacy of VoIP calls. The former studies an approach based on using an anonymization overlay network (such as Tor) with traffic padding (where the overlay knows what traffic to drop because it is marked by the sender). The latter discussed and evaluated (using an analytical model) the use of MIXes to provide strong resistance against traffic analysis for VoIP flows. Their scheme uses dummy traffic, broadcasting, and private information retrieval as building blocks. Srivatsa et al. [247] examined the problem of on-demand construction of QoS-sensitive routes in anonymizing networks.

Elbayoumy and Shepherd [78] propose the use of TEA (Tiny Encryption Algorithm) as a lightweight confidentiality mechanism. Subsequently, they propose an adaptive scheme where the selection of encryption algorithm to be used in protecting traffic is made with consideration of the CPU capabilities of both communicating parties [77, 79].

4.3.1.3 Denial of Service (31 items)

Reynolds and Ghosal [207] describe a multi-layer protection scheme against flood-based application- and transport-layer denial of service (DoS) attacks in VoIP. They use a combination of sensors located across the enterprise network, continuously estimating the deviation from the long-term average of the number of call setup requests and successfully completed handshakes. Similar techniques have been used in detecting TCP SYN flood attacks, with good results. The authors evaluate their scheme via simulation, considering several different types of DoS attacks and recovery models.

Larson et al. [149, 150] experimentally analyzed the impact of distributed denial of service (DDoS) attacks on VoIP call quality. They also established the effectiveness of low-rate denial of service attacks that target specific vulnerabilities and implementation artifacts to cause equipment crashes and reboots. They discuss some of the possible defenses against such attacks and describe Sprint's approach, which uses regional "cleaning centers" which divert suspected attack traffic to a centralized location with numerous screening and mitigation mechanisms available. They recommend that critical VoIP traffic stay on private networks, the use of general DDoS mechanisms as a front-line defense, VoIP-aware DDoS detection and mitigation mechanisms, traffic policing and rate-limiting mechanisms, the use of TCP for VoIP signaling (which makes IP spoofing, and hence anonymous/unfilterable DoS attacks, very difficult), extended protocol compliance checking by VoIP network elements, and the use of authentication where possible.

Bremler-Barr et al. [40] describe de-registration attacks in SIP, wherein an adversary can force a user to be disassociated with the proxy server and registrar, or to even divert that user's calls to any party (including to the attacker). This attack works even when authentication is used, if the adversary can eavesdrop on traffic between the client and the SIP proxy. They demonstrate the attack against several SIP implementations, and propose a protection mechanism that is similar to one-time passwords.

Chen [51] describes a denial of service detection mechanism that models the SIP transaction state machine and identifies attacks by measuring the number of transaction and application errors, the number of transactions per node, and the traffic volume per transaction. If certain thresholds are exceeded, an alert is generated. Chen does not describe how appropriate thresholds can be established, other than to indicate that historical records can be used.

Sengar et al. [224, 226] describe vFDS, an anomaly detection system that seeks to identify flooding denial of service attacks in VoIP. The approach taken is to measure abnormal variations in the relationships between related packet streams using the Hellinger distance, a measure of the deviation between two probability measures. Using synthetic attacks, they show that vFDS can detect flooding attacks that use SYN, SIP, or RTP packets within approximately 1 second of the commencement of an attack, with small impact on call setup latency and voice quality. A similar approach, using Hellinger distance on traffic sketches, is proposed by Tang *et al.* [254], overcoming the limitations of the previous schemes against multi-attribute attacks. Furthermore, their scheme does not require the constant calculation of an accurate threshold (defining "normal" conditions).

Zhang et al. [288] describe a denial of service attack wherein adversaries flood SIP servers with calls involving URIs with DNS names that do not exist. Servers attempting to resolve them will then have to wait until the request times out (either locally or at their DNS server), before they can continue processing the same or another call. This attack works against servers that perform synchronous DNS resolution and only maintain a limited number of execution threads. They experimentally show that as few as 1,000 messages per second can cause a well provisioned synchronous-resolution server to exhibit very high call drops, while simple, single-threaded servers can be starved with even 1 message per second. As a countermeasure, they propose the use of non-blocking DNS caches, which they prototype and evaluate.

Fiedler et al. [84] present VoIP Defender, an open architecture for monitoring SIP traffic, with a primary focus on high-volume denial of service attacks. Their architecture allows for a variety of detection methods to be integrated, and several different attack prevention and mitigation mechanisms to be used. Key design goals include transparency, scalability, extensibility, speed and autonomous operation. Their evaluation of the prototype implementation consists exclusively of performance measurements.

Conner and Nahrstedt [53] describe a semantic-level attack that causes resource exhaustion on stateful SIP proxies by calling parties that (legitimately or in collusion) do not respond. This attack does not require network flooding or other high traffic volume attacks, making it difficult to detect with simple, network-based heuristics used against other types of denial of service attacks. They propose a simple algorithm, called *Random Early Termination* (RET) for releasing reserved resources based on the current state of the proxy (overloaded or not) and the duration of each call's ringing. They implement and evaluate their proposed scheme on a SIP proxy running in a local testbed, showing that it reduces the number of benign call failures when under attack, without incurring measurable overheads when no attack is underway.

Luo et al. [153] experimentally evaluate the susceptibility of SIP to CPU-based denial of service attacks. They use an open-source SIP server in four attack scenarios: basic request flooding, spoofed-nonce flooding (wherein the target server is forced to validate the authenticator in a received message), adaptive-nonce flooding (where the nonce is refreshed periodically by obtaining a new one from the server), and adaptive-nonce flooding with IP spoofing. Their measurements show that these attacks can have a large impact on the quality of service provided by the servers. They propose several countermeasures to mitigate against such attacks, indicating that authentication by itself cannot solve the problem and that, in some circumstances, it can exacerbate its severity. These mitigation mechanisms include lightweight authentication and whitelisting, proper choice of authentication parameters, and binding of nonces to client IP addresses.

Fuchs et al. [89] apply anomaly detection techniques to protect against VoIP-originated denial of service attacks at the phone call level at public safety service centers (e.g., 911 or 112 operators). Specifically, they use call traces from normal operations to determine the level of calls coming from the PSTN, GSM and VoIP networks during normal operation and at disaster time. They then use these profiles to discriminate against VoIP-based DoS attacks by limiting the accepted number of calls that can originate from that domain, building on previous work that identified the network of origin as a potential discriminator [20]. Using call traces from a fire department response center, they evaluate the call response rate against the DoS attack intensity. Their analysis shows that it is possible to identify such attacks early and to avoid false positives if VoIP-originated calls under normal scenarios are less than 27% of total call volume.

Hyun-Soo et al. [126] propose a detection mechanism for de-registration and other call disruption attacks in SIP that is based on message retransmission: when a server receives an unauthenticated (but possibly legitimate) message M that could disturb a call or otherwise deny service to a user, it asks the user's agent to retransmit the last SIP message sent by that agent, as an implicit authenticator. If the retransmission matches M (i.e., this was a legitimate request), the server proceeds with its processing. If the retransmission does not match M, or if multiple retransmissions are received within a short time window (as may be the case when an attacker can eavesdrop on the network link between the SIP proxy and the user, identifying the request for retransmission), M is discarded. However, the scheme requires a new SIP message to signal that a retransmission is needed. Geneiatakis and Lambrinoudakis [91, 93] consider some of the same attacks, and propose mitigation through an additional SIP header that must be included in all messages and can cryptographically validate the authenticity and integrity of control messages.

Ormazabal et al. [181] describe the design and implementation of a SIP-aware, rule-based application-layer firewall that can handle denial of service (and other) attacks in the signaling and media protocols. They use hardware acceleration for the rule matching component, allowing them to achieving filtering rates on the order of hundreds of transactions per second. The SIP-specific rules, combined with state validation of the endpoints, allow the firewall to open precisely the ports needed for only the local and remote addresses involved in a specific session, by decomposing and analyzing the content and meaning of SIP signaling message headers. They experimentally evaluate and validate the behavior of their prototype with a distributed testbed involving synthetic benign and attack traffic generation.

Ehlert et al. [74, 76] propose a two-layer DoS prevention architecture for SIP. The first layer is comprised of a bastion host that protects against well-known network-layer attacks (such as TCP SYN flooding) and SIP-flooding attacks. The second layer is located at the SIP proxy, and is composed of modules that perform signature-based detection of malformed SIP messages and a non-blocking DNS cache to protect against attacks involving SIP URIs with irresolvable DNS names [288]. They conduct a series of evaluations in an experimental testbed, where they validate the effectiveness of their architecture to block or mitigate a number of DoS attacks. Ehlert et al. [73] separate propose and experimentally evaluate (via a testbed) a specification-based intrusion-detection system for denial of service attacks. Geneiatakis et al. [103, 104] use counting Bloom filters to detect messages that are part of a denial of service attack in SIP by determining the normal number of pending sessions for a given system and configuration based on profiling.

Awais et al. [21] describe an anti-DoS architecture based on bio-inspired anomaly detection. They compare their scheme against a cryptography-based mechanism using synthetic traffic. Similar work is described by Rebahi et al. [204]. Akbar and Farooq [9] conduct a comparative evaluation of several evolutionary and non-evolutionary machine learning algorithms using synthetic SIP traffic datasets with different levels of attack intensities and durations. They conclude that different algorithms and settings are best suited for different scenarios. The same authors subsequently apply anomaly detection techniques to identify RTP fuzzing attacks that seek to cause server crashes through malformed packet headers and payloads [10]. They investigate several different classifiers, analyzing their accuracy and performance using synthetic RTP traces. Nassar et al. [176] use support vector machine (SVM) classifiers on 38 distinct features in SIP traffic to identify SPIT and DoS traffic. Their experiments using SIP traffic traces show good performance and high detection accuracy.

Rafique et al. [195] analyze the robustness and reliability of SIP servers under DoS attacks. They launch a number of synthesized attacks against four well-known SIP proxy servers (OpenSER, PartySIP, OpenSBC, and MjServer). Their results demonstrate the ease with which SIP servers can be overloaded with call requests, causing such performance metrics as Call Completion Rate, Call Establishment Latency, Call Rejection Ration and Number of Retransmitted Requests to deteriorate rapidly as attack volume increases, sometimes with as few as 1,000 packets/second. As an extreme case of such attacks large volumes of INVITE messages can even cause certain implementations to crash. While valuable in documenting the susceptibility to such attacks, this work proposes no defense strategies or directions.

Akbar et al. [11] conduct an analysis of three anomaly detection algorithms for detecting flood attacks in IMS: adaptive threshold, cumulative sum, and Hellinger distance. They use synthetic traffic data to determine the detection accuracy of these algorithms in the context of a SIP server being flooded with SIP messages.

Battistello [28] introduces a DoS-resistant protocol for authenticated call establishment with key exchange across different domains.

4.3.1.4 Service Abuse (7 items)

Truong et al. [259] describe a rules-based intrusion detection system for H.323 that uses an FSM model to detect unexpected messages, aimed at identifying illegitimate RAS (Registration, Admission and Status) messages being forwarded to a H.323 gatekeeper.

Kotulski and Mazurczyk [142, 163, 164] propose the use of steganographic and digital watermarking to embed additional information into SIP traffic to provide stronger origin authentication and content integrity guarantees in a bandwidth-sensitive manner. Their scheme encodes the necessary information into unused fields in the IP, UDP and RTP protocol headers, and also into the transmitted voice.

Zhang et al. [289] present a number of exploitable vulnerabilities in SIP that can manipulate billing records in a number of ways, showing their applicability against real commercial VoIP providers. Their focus is primarily on attacks that create billing inconsistencies, e.g., customers being charged for service they did not receive, or over-charged for service received. Some of these attacks require a man-in-the-middle capability, while others only require some prior interaction with the target (e.g., receiving a call from the victim SIP phone device).

Abdelnur et al. [5] use AVISPA to identify a protocol-level vulnerability in the way SIP handles authentication [249]. AVISPA is a model checker for validating security protocols and applications using a high-level protocol specification and security-goals language that gets compiler into an intermediate format that can be consumed by a number of lower-level checkers. The attack is possible with the SIP Digest Authentication, whereby an adversary can reuse another party's credentials to obtain unauthorized access to SIP or PSTN services (such as calling a premium or international phone line). This attack is possible because authentication may be requested in response to an INVITE message at any time during a call, and the responder may issue an INVITE message during a call either automatically (because of timer expirations) or through a user action (e.g., placing the caller on hold in order to do a call transfer). While the solution is simple, it requires changes possibly to all end-device SIP implementations.

Geneiatakis et al. [101] address the problem of billing attacks against telephony service providers and their users. They propose an authentication-based scheme that leverages the existing Authentication, Authorization and Accounting (AAA) infrastructure operated by the service provider to provide the latter with explicit and non-repudiable call confirmation by the call initiator. However, the scheme has not been implemented or evaluated, experimentally or formally.

4.3.2 Additional Categories (134 items)

We now classify the remainder of the surveyed work (55% of the total) using the following categories: Overviews (19.7%), Field Studies and Analysis (4.9%), Performance Analysis (5.7%), Authentication Protocols (6.1%), Architecture (7.8%) Middleboxes (4.5%) Intrusion Detection (4.5%), and Miscellaneous (0.8%).

4.3.2.1 Overviews and Surveys (50 items)

There is a considerable body of work focusing on surveying and summarizing risks and threats in SIP, and describing existing work on defense mechanisms.

General overviews (42 items)

Ackermann et al. [7] describe threats in VoIP, focusing on specific attacks and vulnerabilities as case studies. Hunter [125], Batchvarov [27], Bradbury [39], and Chau [50] provide summaries of specific security concerns in VoIP.

Sicker and Lookabaugh [233] discuss threats in VoIP and the need for security to be integrated at design and deployment time. Vuong and Bai [265] provide a brief survey of the types of intrusion detection systems that can be used to monitor for specific types of attacks in VoIP.

Geneiatakis et al. [96] describe how SQL injection attacks can be launched through SIP, by including partial SQL statements in certain fields of SIP protocol messages that are likely to be used in subsequent database operations (e.g., parts of the SIP URI in the To: field may be used to look up the location of the user receiving the call). They demonstrate the attack in a lab experiment, and briefly discuss the applicability of general SQL injection defense mechanisms in a SIP environment.

Tucker [262] gives an overview of SIP and H.323, and briefly mentions some security concerns (with an emphasis on denial of service). Posegga and Seedorf [188] offer a similar threat analysis. Edelson [72] discusses denial of service, SPIT, eavesdropping and security of emergency calls, before talking about the particular requirements of VoIP in wireless. She concludes with a brief discussion of intrusion detection for VoIP. Albers et al. [13] gives a high-level overview of the types of vulnerabilities that SIP-based systems may be exposed to, and discusses the capabilities and limitations of a number of commercially available (as of 2005) SIP intrusion prevention and testing systems. In a related publication, McGann and Sicker [165] argue that several of the VoIP security tools available in 2005 did not cover the extent of known vulnerabilities, do not provide the coverage claimed by the developers, and were not user-friendly. A short overview of some SIP security mechanisms is given by Geneiatakis et al. [94].

Cao and Malik [44, 45] examine the vulnerabilities that arise from introducing VoIP technologies into the communications systems in critical infrastructure applications. They examine the usual threats and vulnerabilities, and discuss mitigation techniques. They conclude by providing some recommendations and best practices to operators of such systems.

Allain [15] discusses the security challenges in VoIP environments, focusing on a couple of specific issues to highlight the tradeoffs. Adelsbach et al. [8] provide a comprehensive description of SIP and H.323, a list of threats across all networking layers, and various protection mechanisms. A similar analysis was published by the US National Institute of Standards and Technology (NIST) [144]. An updated summary, with practical recommendations to users and operators is provided by Walsh and Kuhn [266]. Anwar et al. [16] identify some areas where the NIST report remains incomplete: counter-intuitive results with respect to the relative performance of encryption and hash algorithms, the non-use of the standardized Mean Opinion Score to evaluate call quality, and the lack of anticipation of RTP-based denial of service. They then propose the use of design patterns to address the problems of secure traversal of firewalls and NAT boxes, detecting and mitigating DoS attacks in VoIP, and securing VoIP against eavesdropping.

Geneiatakis et al. [97] also survey a number of SIP security vulnerabilities. Geneiatakis et al. [102] categorize potential attacks on VoIP services, and provide recommendations and guidelines for protecting the infrastructure. They use ontologies to represent these recommendations, and first-order logic to translate them to a unified security policy for VoIP.

Me and Verdone [166] describe the security threats and high-level vulnerabilities in SIP when used in 802.11 or other similar wireless environments. Singhai and Sahoo [236] describe the risks of VoIP technologies (focusing on SIP and H.323) and compare them with the public switched telephony network (PSTN). Rippon [210] provides a laundry list of threats and mitigation techniques for VoIP systems. Brief descriptions of some VoIP-related threats are given by Hung and Martin [123, 124] and Zandi et al. [284].

Xin [279] provides a somewhat more detailed overview of VoIP-related security concerns. Persky gives a very detailed description of several VoIP vulnerabilities [184]. Quinten et al. [191] survey the various techniques for preventing and reducing SPIT, offering some suggestions as to possible combinations that increase overall blocking effectiveness. Hansen and Woodward [116] overview threats in VoIP environments and recommend that VoIP and data networks be logically or physically separated. James and Woodward [129] propose a security framework for end users of VoIP technologies, combining a number of commonly available mechanisms and recommendations.

Butcher et al. [42] overview security issues and mechanisms for VoIP systems, focusing on security-oriented operational practices by VoIP providers and operators. Such practices include the separation of VoIP and data traffic by using VLANs and similar techniques, the use of integrity and authentication for configuration bootstrapping of VoIP devices, authentication of signaling via TLS or IPsec, and the use of media encryption. They briefly describe how two specific commercial systems implement such practices, and propose some directions for future research.

A comprehensive discussion of threats and security solutions is given by Thermos and Takanen [258]. Kurmus and Garet [146] summarize a number of threats and specific vulnerabilities using actual attack tools.

Sisalem et al. [239] provide an in-depth description of SIP and IMS, discussing the security mechanisms available in each part of the architecture. The focus particularly on the DoS and SPIT threats, also describing some available countermeasures.

Gurbani and Kolesnikov [110] discuss in depth and compare SDES, DTLS-SRTP, and ZRTP in terms features supported (e.g., conferencing, PSTN calling) and security features/weaknesses (*e.g.*, susceptibility to man-in-the-middle attacks and key leakage). They conclude that all three are suitable, but they each offer a feature or suppress a vulnerability that the others do not.

Keromytis [136, 137, 138] surveys over 200 vulnerabilities in SIP implementations that were disclosed in the CVE database from 1999 to 2009. He classifies these vulnerabilities along several dimensions, including the VoIPSA threat taxonomy, the traditional Confidentiality/Integrity/Availability concerns, and a Protocol/Implementation/Configuration axis. He finds that the various types of denial of service attacks constitute the majority of disclosed vulnerabilities, over 90% of which were due to implementation problems and 7% due to configuration.

SPIT (6 items)

The SPIDER project (SPam over Internet telephony Detection sERvice) released a public report [202] providing an overview of SPIT threats and the relevant European legal framework (both on an EU and national basis). The second public report [159] focuses on SPIT detection and prevention, summarizing some of the work done in this space and defining criteria for evaluating the efficiency of anti-SPIT mechanisms. The report classifies prior work according to fulfillment of these criteria, expanding on the relative strengths and weaknesses of each approach.

Dritsas et al. [66] and Marias et al. [158] survey the risks of SPIT in SIP, the latter also taking into consideration feedback from SIP operators. They then classify a number of previously proposed anti-SPIT mechanisms along a prevent/detect/handle axis. Dritsas *et al.* [67] survey a number of anti-SPIT mechanisms and techniques against a set of criteria that they argue is needed to identify a call as SPIT.

d'Heureuse et al. [62] give an overview of the various anti-SPIT efforts in standardization bodies and propose an architecture for dealing with unwanted communications composed of 5 stages: non-intrusive pre-call message analysis, interaction with the caller, pre-connection callee feedback, call content analysis and real-time callee feedback, and post-call callee feedback.

Denial of Service (1 item)

Sisalem et al. [238] give an overview of SIP-based DoS attacks, looking at a couple of specific scenarios. They provide some recommendations to implementors of VoIP systems that mitigate some of these attacks.

P2P SIP (1 item)

Seedorf [220] overviews the security challenges in peer-to-peer (P2P) SIP. Threats specific to P2P-SIP include subversion of the identity-mapping scheme (which is specific to the overlay network used as a substrate), attacks on the overlay network routing scheme, bootstrapping communications in the presence of malicious first-contact nodes, identity enforcement (Sybil attacks), traffic analysis and privacy violation by intermediate nodes, and free riding by nodes that refuse to route calls or otherwise participate in the protocol other than to obtain service for themselves.

4.3.2.2 Field Studies and System/Protocol Analysis (12 items)

Wieser et al. [271] extend the PROTOS testsuite [132] with a SIP-specific analysis fuzzing module. They then test their system against a number of commercial SIP implementations, finding critical vulnerabilities in all of them [57].

Berson [32] conducted an evaluation of the Skype system under contract by Skype itself, allowing him access to the source code. The evaluation focused primarily on the cryptographic protocols and algorithms used, and did not discover any significant issues. Baset and Schulzrinne [26] performed a black-box analysis of Skype, identifying some characteristics of the underlying protocol. Biondi and Desclaux [38] dissected the Skype binary in detail, exposing the extensive anti-reverse engineer and anti-debugging mechanisms built in the program. Their analysis identified a small number of vulnerabilities (including a buffer overflow).

Thermos and Hadsall [257] survey a number of Small Office Home Office (SOHO) VoIP gateways and related equipment, as provided by 3 different commercial VoIP providers with different corporate profiles and customer bases. Their analysis looks at four key factors: manageability, node security, signaling security, and media security. They find numerous problems, including insecure access to the web-based management interface, default passwords and inappropriate services, lack of encryption to protect signaling and media, and low-level implementation issues (e.g., presumed buffer overflow vulnerabilities and fuzzing-induced crashes). A similar survey by Scholz [218] looks at protocol and device problems and vulnerabilities at a medium-size German ISP with high rate of VoIP adoption. He focuses on intentional and unintentional denial of service attacks, problems in customer-premises equipment (e.g., SIP phones), and protocol-independent issues. A number of problems are found, including DoS through call forks, misconfigured devices, and lawful-interception evasion, among others.

INRIA has been conducting a multi-thrust effort to apply testing and fuzzing toward identifying vulnerabilities in SIP protocols [6], implementations [4] and deployed systems [2, 3]. It is worth noting that this work has resulted in a number of vulnerability disclosures in the Common Vulnerabilities and Exposures (CVE) database and elsewhere.

Gupta and Shmatikov [108] formally analyze the security of the VoIP protocol stack, including SIP, SDP, ZRTP, MIKEY, SDES, and SRTP. Their analysis uncovers a number of flaws, most of which derive from subtle inconsistencies in the assumptions made in designing the different protocols. These attacks include a replay attack in SDES that completely break content protection, a man-in-the-middle attack in ZRTP, and a (perhaps theoretical) weakness in the key derivation process used in MIKEY. They also show several minor weaknesses and vulnerabilities in all protocols, primarily enabling denial of service attacks. Floroiu and Sisalem [87] also conduct a comparative analysis of the security aspects of DTLS, ZRTP, MIKEY and SDES. They describe a number of possible attacks against these protocols, and propose mitigation approaches in some cases.

4.3.2.3 Performance Analysis (14 items)

Reason and Messerchmitt [198], in one of the earliest works on the subject of the performance impact of security mechanisms on VoIP, looked specifically at the error-expansion properties of encryption and their effect on voice quality. They analytically derive the post-decryption Bit Error Rate (BER) relative to the pre-encryption BER for block and stream ciphers, and analyze the effect of error-expansion mitigation techniques, such as the use of forward error correction, on quality of service. They discuss an error-robust encryption scheme that is analogous to self-synchronizing ciphers.

Elbayoumi and Shepherd [81] conduct a performance comparison of block and stream cipher encryption in the context of securing VoIP calls. They analyze the impact of each on end-to-end delay and subjective quality of perceived voice. A broader view at several performance-impacting parameters is given by the same authors in a concurrent paper at the same journal [80].

Salsano et al. [215] give an overview of the various SIP security mechanisms (as of 2002), focusing particularly on the authentication component. They conduct an evaluation of the processing costs of SIP calls that involve authentication, under different transport, authentication and encryption scenarios. They show that a call using TLS and authentication is 2.56 times more expensive than the simplest possible SIP configuration (UDP, no security). However, a fully protected call takes only 54% longer to complete than a configuration that is more representative than the basic one but still offers no security; the same fully-protected call has the same processing cost if it is transported over TCP with no encryption (TLS). Of the overhead, approximately 70% is attributed to message parsing and 30% to cryptographic processing. With the advent of Datagram TLS (DTLS) [172], it is possible that encryption and integrity for SIP can be had for all configurations (UDP or TCP) at no additional cost.

Barbieri et al. [24] find that when using VoIP over IPsec, performance can drop by up to 63%; however, it is questionable whether these results still hold, given the use of hardware accelerators and the more efficient AES algorithm in IPsec. Simulation-based work by Ranganathan and Kilmartin [197] shows that the use of IPsec with pre-established Security Associations (SAs) increases SIP call setup time by 1.4% and media (voice) transfer by 1.6%. However, when taking into consideration the delay in establishing SAs for the first time using a dynamic key-agreement protocol such as IKE [118] or IKEv2 [133], the call setup delay can increase dramatically. They identify encryption engine queuing delays as a potential concern, as call volumes increase.

A conclusion similar to Salsano et al. [215] is reached by Bilien [35] and Bilien et al. [36, 37], who study the overhead in SIP call setup latency when using end-to-end and hop-by-hop security mechanisms. They consider protocols such as MIKEY, S/MIME, SRTP, TLS, and IPsec, concluding that the overall penalty of using full-strength cryptography is low.

Xiao and Zarrella [278] conduct an experimental evaluation of the impact of security mechanisms on VoIP in wireless environments with a specific voice codec.

They specifically look at how the use of IPsec and WEP affect the Mean Opinion Score, packet loss, and delay of VoIP calls in 802.11 networks. They find that WEP has a bigger impact on packet loss than IPsec, but the latter can cause larger packet delays and fewer but more extreme voice artifacts (disturbances) in the call.

Also in the context of VoIP for wireless networks, Lakay and Agbinya [148] summarize similar experiments that show SIP security mechanism processing is responsible for 80% of the call setup delay when using stateless proxies, and 45% for stateful proxies.

Eun-Chul et al. [82], evaluate via simulation the costs of different security protocols (TLS, DTLS and IPsec) with respect to call setup delay using different transport protocols (TCP, UDP and SCTP). They conclude that the most efficient combinations, DTLS/UDP and IPsec/UDP, approximately double the call setup delay. However, since the analysis is purely simulation-based, their results are sensitive to the configured relative costs for processing the various protocols.

Shen et al. [229] also study the performance impact of using TLS as a transport protocol for SIP. In their experiments using a testbed, they use profiling at various system levels (application, library, and kernel), and decompose the costs at a fine level of granularity. They determine that use of TLS can reduce performance by a factor of up to 20 (when compared with the unsecured SIP-over-UDP). The main overhead factor is the cost of RSA signatures during session negotiation, while symmetric key operations impose a relatively small cost. They recommend that operators amortize the setup cost over long-lived connections. Finally, they provide a cost model for provisioning SIP-over-TLS servers, predicting an average performance overhead of 15% under a suggested system configuration.

Rebahi et al. [203] analyze the performance of RSA as used in SIP for authentication and identity management (via public-key certificates and digital signatures), and describe the use of Elliptic Curve DSA (ECDSA) within this context to improve performance. Using ECDSA, their prototype can handle from 2 to 8 times as many call setup requests per second, with the gap widening as key sizes increase.

4.3.2.4 Authentication Protocols (15 items)

Buschel [41] argues for integrated authentication between User Agents and all elements of a SIP infrastructure. Over the years, a number of authentication schemes aiming to replace Digest Authentication have been proposed, using such basic blocks as Diffie Hellman [282], Elliptic Curve Diffie Hellman (ECDH) [70], Elliptic Curve Discrete Logarithm Problem (ECDLP) [283], nonces [260], PKI [173, 244] hash functions [122], and others [49], not all of them secure [151].

Cao and Jennings [43] propose a new mechanism for authenticating the responding user's identity in SIP without exposing said identity to untrusted intermediate elements. Their scheme requires additional headers in SIP messages, and has not been implemented or evaluated.

Insu and Keecheon [128] propose a secret key based mechanism to reduce the performance requirements of using public key certificates to protect signaling (e.g., with TLS) in an enterprise VoIP environment.

Schmidt et al. [217] suggest that administration overheads for implementing strong authentication in SIP could be lowered by grouping users with the same function or role (e.g., agents in a calling center). They propose a proxy-based mechanism for implementing a form of "certificate sharing" among a group of users, without exposing the corresponding private key to any of them. They demonstrate feasibility of the scheme by implementing it in the NIST SIP proxy, with no further evaluation.

Wang and Zhang [268] discuss an authentication and key agreement mechanism for SIP that uses certificate-less public-key cryptography. Certificate-less public-key cryptography [12] is a variant of identity-based cryptography (where the public key of an entity is its public identity); here, the public key for an entity is generated collaboratively between that entity and a trusted third party in such a way that the public key can be verified by any other entity that knows the public parameters under which the trusted third party operates. Compared to previous proposals that used identity-based cryptography [209], their scheme does not require that the trusted third party

4.3.2.5 Architectures (19 items)

Singh and Vuong [235] use a mobile agent framework to collect and correlate events from various network components, toward detecting a number of attacks. The stated advantages of their approach are that it does not require a new protocol for exchanging event information and that mitigation and recovery capabilities can be implemented by extending the framework and the agents, with no changes to the VoIP protocols. They also propose using user behavior profiles to detect anomalous behavior. They describe the operation of their system in a number of attack scenarios, including protocol-based denial of service, call hijacking, packet flooding, and abnormal call patterns.

Casola et al. [47, 48] suggest the use of a policy-based approach to design secure VoIP infrastructures. The policies express security goals in measurable terms; suggested infrastructure designs can then be evaluated against these policies to determine whether the goals are met to an acceptable degree.

Wu et al. [275] design an intrusion detection system, called SCIDIVE, that is specific to VoIP environments. Specifically, SCIDIVE aims to detect different classes of intrusions, can operate with different viewpoints (on clients, proxies, or servers), and takes into consideration both signaling (i.e., SIP) and media-transfer protocols (e.g., RTP). SCIDIVE's ability to correlate cross-protocol behavior, theoretically allows for detection of more complex attacks. However, the system is rules-based, which limits its effectiveness against new/unknown attacks. The primary evaluation (conducted on a small testbed) consists of four simple cross-protocol attacks, which would have evaded other contemporary, non-specialized intrusion detection systems. In follow-on work, Apte et al. [17, 276] develop SPACEDIVE, a VoIP-specific intrusion detection system that allows for correlation of events among distributed rules-based detectors. They demonstrate the ability of SPACEDIVE to detect certain classes of attacks using a simple SIP environment with two domains, and compare it with SCIDIVE.

Martin and Hung [161] discuss a high-level policy for VoIP applications, intended to guide the implementation, configuration, and use of VoIP systems.

SNOCER[1], a project funded by the European Union, is "investigating approaches for overcoming temporal network, hardware and software failures and ensuring the high availability of the offered VoIP services based on low cost distributed concepts." The first public project report [237] provides an overview of VoIP infrastructure components and the threats that must be addressed (staying primarily at the protocol and network level, and avoiding implementation issues with the exception of SQL injection), along with possible defense mechanisms. There is also discussion on scalable service provisioning (replication, redundancy, backups etc.), toward providing reliability and fault tolerance. The second public project report [58] describes an architecture for protecting against malformed messages and related attacks using specification-based intrusion detection, protocol message verification, and redundancy. They use ontologies to describe SIP vulnerabilities, to allow for easy updating of the monitoring components (IDS) [92].

Niccolini et al. [178] design an intrusion detection/intrusion prevention system architecture for use with SIP. Their system uses both knowledge-based and behavior-based detection, arranged as a series in that order. They develop a prototype implementation using the open-source Snort IDS. They evaluate the effectiveness of their system in an attack scenario by measuring the mean end-to-end delay of legitimate SIP traffic in the presence of increasing volumes of malformed SIP INVITE messages.

Marshall et al. [160] describe the AT&T VoIP security architecture. They divide VoIP equipment into three classes: trusted, trusted-but-vulnerable, and untrusted. The latter consists of the customer premises equipment, which is outside the control of the carrier. The trusted domain includes all the servers necessary to provide VoIP service. Between the two sit various border and security elements, that are responsible for protecting the trusted devices while permitting legitimate communications to proceed. They describe the interactions among the various components, and the security mechanisms used in protecting these interactions.

Sher and Magedanz [230] describe a security architecture for IMS service delivery platforms, focusing on time-independent attacks (e.g., software vulnerabilities). The key element of their proposed approach is an intrusion detection and prevention system that inspects all incoming and outgoing SIP messages to the IMS application servers, applying rules that detect and mitigate specific attacks. A brief performance evaluation shows that a prototype can operate with acceptable delay parameters.

Ding and Su [65] propose the combination of specification-based intrusion detection with anomaly detection techniques and attack-specific methods using hierarchical colored Petri nets.

---

[1] http://www.snocer.org/

Nassar et al. [175] advocate the use of SIP-specific honeypots to catch attacks targeting the Internet telephony systems, protocols and applications. They design and implement such a honeypot system, and explore the use of a statistical engine for identifying attacks and other misbehavior, based on training on legitimate traces of SIP traffic. The engine is based on their prior work that uses Bayesian-based inference. The resulting SIP honeypot effort is largely exploratory, with performance and effectiveness evaluations left for future work. In follow-on work, Nassar et al. [174] describe an intrusion detection and prevention architecture for VoIP that integrates SIP honeypots and an application-layer event correlation engine.

Barry and Chan [25] describe a host-based intrusion detection architecture for SIP that combines specification-based and signature-based detection, and allows for the correlation of information across modules to identify cross-protocol attacks. They conduct a simulation-based evaluation using OMNeT++ to determine detection accuracy and performance impact.

Rieck et al. [208] apply machine learning techniques to detecting anomalous SIP messages, incorporating a "self-learning" component by allowing for periodic retraining of the anomaly detector using traffic that has been flagged as normal. The features used for clustering are based on n-grams and on tokenization of the SIP protocol. To prevent training attacks, wherein an adversary "trains" the anomaly detector to accept malicious inputs as legitimate, they employ randomization (choosing random samples for the training set), sanitization [54], and verification (by comparing the output of the new and old training models). Their experimental prototype was shown to handle 70 Mbps of SIP traffic, while providing a 99% detection rate with no false positives.

Dantu et al. [61] describe a comprehensive VoIP security architecture, composed of components distributed across the media gateway controller, the proxy server(s), the IP PBX, and end-user equipment. These components explicitly exchange information toward better training of filters, and creating and maintaining whitelists/blacklists. Implicit feedback is also provided through statistical analysis of interactions (e.g., call frequency and duration). The architecture also provisions for a recovery mechanism that incorporates explicit feedback and quarantining.

4.3.2.6 Middleboxes (11 items)

Reynolds and Ghosal [206] describe a VoIP-aware middlebox architecture that integrates the enterprise firewall, media gateway, and intrusion detection facilities to allow the secure operation of dynamic VoIP applications. The problem of firewall and NAT traversal by VoIP protocols has been the subject of some research [147, 211, 234, 251], generally involving some kind of signaling (whether in-band or out-of-band) between the end-device and the middlebox.

Bessis et al. [34] discuss the necessary features of a SIP-specific firewall, juxtaposing them with specific threats to SIP messages at each network layer (data link, network, transport and session). They propose a simple, hardware-accelerated SIP-proxy as a front-end SIP firewall and argue that this approach would block most of the attacks.

Gurbani et al. [111] propose an mechanism whereby proxies create an overlay network between user agents. This network is used for rendezvous/coordination purposes only. Once user agents establish a session, the proxies become transparent traffic forwarders, with the user agents communicating over an end-to-end secure session. This approach allows users to communicate without exposing (as much) private information to proxies, at the cost of requiring a PKI and a new message extension.

Sengar et al. [222, 223, 225] examine the problem of cross-infrastructure vulnerabilities created by bridging VoIP and PSTN networks. They outline a high-level architecture that integrates firewall-like functionality with trust management, signaling encryption and authentication, and intrusion detection.

Ehlert et al. [75] describe a rule-reduction algorithm for improving the performance of firewalls operating in busy VoIP environments, in balance with security requirements. Their algorithm works by merging similar single-mapped rules into a more general rule, then dropping less important rules, and finally calculating the accuracy of the new ruleset. If needed, their algorithm re-iterates until an acceptable solution is achieved.

4.3.2.7 Intrusion Detection (11 items)

Mandjes et al. [156, 157] describe the use of statistical techniques to identify anomalies in VoIP networks. Their work is primarily directed at non-adversarial anomalies, although certain attacks (such as denial of service) would also be detected by their scheme.

Geneiatakis et al. [95, 99] discuss malformed-message attacks against SIP servers and equipment, primarily depending on the PROTOS testsuite for SIP implementations [132]. To detect such attacks, they propose building an intrusion detection system that leverages the SIP syntax grammar [212] to decompose incoming messages, and a grammar for specifying rules that check whether specific constraints are being violated (or specific conditions met) [98, 100]. In subsequent work, Geneiatakis and Keromytis [90] apply entropy theory and "itself information" to the problem of identifying anomalies in a stream of SIP messages.

However, Hantehzadeh et al. [117] point out that the most approaches to anomaly detection in SIP use datasets with large differences between anomalous and normal messages, which make them easy to detect. An analysis using a dataset with minimal such differences (while maintaining the distinction between malicious and normal messages) indicates that existing classification schemes do not perform as well. They propose feature reduction techniques to enhance these classification schemes even on "trickier" datasets. Similar results, focusing specifically on the performance of classifiers using Euclidean distance, are discussed by Mehta et al. [167].

Sengar et al. [225] model the protocol state machine of individual SIP nodes (derived from the SIP specification) and inter-node interactions, in order to have a complete picture of the overall system state towards detecting anomalous behavior and attacks. This is particularly important in VoIP, since nodes can interact in many ways, and with several other nodes during a call and throughout their operation. They conduct a performance evaluation to determine the overhead added to call setup and media transfer by their system, and its overall scalability. While their system can identify known attacks (for which attack patterns can be specified) with high accuracy and low false positives, detecting previously unknown attacks depends on the fidelity of the protocol state machines. This problem is left for future work.

Seo et al. [227] develop a stateful intrusion detection system for SIP, modeling SIP state transitions to match the expected state of the monitored SIP entities. Their system allows the specification of rules that match attacks and misbehavior based not only on the content of the communications but also on the state of the SIP call and of the proxies.

4.3.2.8 Miscellaneous (2 items)

Cao et al. [46] describe how to transparently add information in SIP and H.323 messages such that calls can be tracked across the network. A similar approach, leveraging watermarking of VoIP content, was previously described by Steinebach et al. [250].

5
Comparative Analysis

Figures 17 and 19 show the breakdown of the various research papers across the VoIPSA and extended classifications, respectively. For easy visual comparison, we include again the breakdown of known vulnerabilities across from Sec. 3, shown here in Figure 18. As can be easily seen, there are large discrepancies between research focus and known vulnerabilities (and, presumably, needs for further work), specifically in the areas of denial of service and social threats. The latter seems over-represented, a fact perhaps explained by our prior experience with email spam and the concomitant desire to avoid it in the VoIP realm. Furthermore, we should point out that some research on denial of service prevention and mitigation is more general than VoIP, and thus should (in principle) be included here.

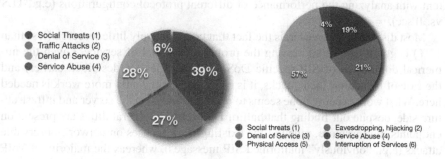

Fig. 17 Classification of research papers according to VoIPSA taxonomy

Fig. 18 Vulnerability breakdown based on VoIPSA taxonomy

When we look at the combined research space (both VoIPSA and extended classifications), the situation changes significantly (mostly for the worse).

Considering the research work we have surveyed, we can see that out of a total of 245 publications, almost 20% concern themselves with an overview of the problem space and of solutions — a figure we believe is reasonable, considering the enormity of the problem space and the speed of change in the protocols, standards, and

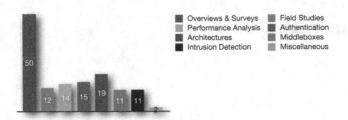

Fig. 19 Classification of research papers according to extended taxonomy

implementations. We also see a considerable amount of effort (roughly 20%) going toward addressing SPIT. While SPIT does not appear to be a major issue with VoIP users at this point, our past and current experiences with email spam and telemarketing seems to provide sufficient motivation for research in this area. Most of the work is focused on identifying SPIT calls and callers based on behavioral traits, although a number of other approaches are under exploration (e.g., CAPTCHAs and real-time content analysis). One of the problems is the lack of a good corpus of data for experimentation and validation of the proposed techniques.

We were also not surprised to see a sizable portion of research (over 15%) directed at design, analysis (both security- and performance-oriented), and attacking of cryptographic protocols as used in VoIP. The cryptographic research community appears to be reasonably comfortable in proposing tweaks and minor improvements to the basic authentication mechanisms, and the systems community appears content with analyzing the performance of different protocol configurations (e.g., TLS vs. IPsec).

Most distressing, however, is the fact that comparatively little research (less than 13%) is going toward addressing the problem of denial of service. Given the numerical dominance of SIP-specific DoS vulnerabilities (as described earlier) and the ease of launching such attacks, it is clear that significantly more work is needed here. What work is being done seems to primarily focus on the server and infrastructure side, despite our finding that half of DoS-related vulnerabilities are present on endpoints. Furthermore, much of the existing work focuses on network-observable attacks (e.g., "obviously" malformed SIP messages), whereas the majority of VoIP DoS vulnerabilities are the result of implementation failures. More generally, additional work is needed in strengthening implementations, rather than introducing middleboxes and network intrusion detection systems, whose effectiveness has been shown to be limited in other domains; taking a black box approach in securing VoIP systems is, in our opinion, not going to be sufficient.

Also disconcerting is the lack of research (2.8%) in addressing service abuse threats, considering the visibility of large fraud incidents [143, 255, 256].

In general, we found little work that took a "big picture" view of the VoIP security problem. What cross-cutting architectures have been proposed focus primarily on intrusion detection. Work is needed to address cross-implementation and cross-protocol problems, above and beyond the few efforts along those lines in the intrusion detection space.

Finally, we note that none of the surveyed works addressed the problem of configuration management. While such problems represent only 7% of known vulnerabilities, configuration issues are easy to overlook and are likely under-represented in our previous analysis due to the nature of vulnerability reporting.

5.1 Recommendations for Securing VoIP Systems

The large majority of disclosed threats focused on DoS attacks based on implementation issues. While fault-tolerance techniques (such as replication) can be applied in the case of servers, it is less clear how to provide similar levels of protection at acceptable cost and usability to end user devices. Unfortunately, the ease with which mass DoS attacks can be launched over the network against client devices means that they represent an attractive venue for attackers to achieve the same impact.

Code injection attacks in their various forms remain a problem, despite considerable progress in creating defenses. We need to do a better job at deploying and using these defenses where possible, and devising new techniques suitable for the constrained environments that some vulnerable VoIP devices represent.

Weak default configurations are also a big problem, as they do across a large class of consumer and enterprise products and software. The situation is likely to be much worse in the real world, considering the complexity of securely configuring a system with as many components as VoIP. Vendors must make an effort to provide secure-by-default configurations, and to educate users how best to protect their systems. Administrators are in need of tools to analyze their existing configurations for vulnerabilities. While some tools dynamically test network components (e.g., firewalls), we need tools that work higher in the protocol and application stack. Furthermore, we need ways of validating configurations across multiple components and protocols.

Finally, there is simply no excuse for protocol-level vulnerabilities. While there exist techniques for analyzing and verifying security protocols, they do not seem to cope well with complexity. Aside from using such tools and continuing their development, protocol designers and standardization committees must consider the impact of their decisions on system implementers, *i.e.*, whether it is likely that a feature or aspect of the protocol is likely to be misunderstood and/or mis-implemented. Unfortunately, while simpler protocols are desirable, they seem incompatible with the trends we have observed in standardization bodies.

Network administrators can and must be proactive. Concrete steps to protect VoIP systems include but are not limited to:

- Stay up to date with firmware updates and security news about the devices deployed in your network. It is easy to overlook the fact that a VoIP hardphone may require a software update, just as servers and desktops do.

- Change the default/administrator authentication credentials in all devices and services! Make sure you cover all services running in each device (e.g., the web-based management interface).
- Use any of a number of free or commercial SIP fuzzing tools, especially before initial roll-out of VoIP services, and after each firmware/software update. Do this both against end devices (hardphones and softphones) and servers.
- Make it your business to know what services each VoIP device is running. Do not trust the vendor to have produced a locked-down system—several misconfiguration-induced vulnerabilities came from leftover services running on the device. A simple port-scan will typically reveal such problems. If a service is not absolutely necessary, stop it; if that is not possible, block it at the firewall and complain to the vendor.
- Take steps to harden your VoIP servers. This may involve using obscure OS security features, or a different OS altogether. If possible, consider using a redundant server configuration with different operating systems running the same application server. (Using different application servers would be ideal, but impractical over the long run due to incompatibilities and configuration drift.)

    - If you use server redundancy, make sure to test it periodically! There's nothing worse than discovering your secondary server is misconfigured while your primary server is compromised[1].

- Harden/protect the infrastructure on which your VoIP services rely on. Specific services that merit attention include DNS, DHCP, and TFTP. This involves many of the steps mentioned above, for each of these services.
- Limit arbitrary access to VoIP devices. While this seems at odds with the basic premise of VoIP, it is possible to channel communications through media gateways. While this risks introducing some scalability problems, it also offers the opportunity to monitor traffic for abnormal behavior and to block some types of attacks against end devices.

    - Along the same lines, you may also want to consider putting all your VoIP traffic into a different VLAN, especially if VLAN-port configurations can be frozen (admittedly a difficult proposition in many environments).

- When possible, enable TLS authentication and encryption for SIP signaling and use SRTP for media encryption. While the use of SRTP in particular is not widespread, the benefits appear to outweigh the (performance-related) drawbacks.

While there is no guarantee that the above steps will prevent a compromise (or that they are complete), they would have helped against most of the disclosed vulnerabilities we examined. The bottom line is that, while the situation with respect to VoIP security is currently bleak, there are steps you can take to protect your infrastructure today.

---

[1] In reality, there are many things worse than this. Nonetheless, it is a very unpleasant situation.

6
Conclusions

We can draw some preliminary conclusions with respect to threats and focus areas for future research based on the data examined so far. These can be summarized as follows:

1. The large majority of disclosed threats focused on denial of services attacks based on implementation issues. While fault-tolerance techniques can be applied in the case of servers (replication, hot standby, Byzantine fault tolerance, etc.), it is less clear how to provide similar levels of protection at acceptable cost and usability to end user devices. Unfortunately, the easy with which mass DoS attacks can be launched over the network against client devices means that they represent an attractive venue for attackers to achieve the same impact.
2. Code injection attacks in their various forms (buffer overflow, cross-site scripting, SQL injection, etc.) remain a problem. While a number of techniques have been developed, we need to do a better job at deploying and using them where possible, and devising new techniques suitable for the constrained environments that some vulnerable VoIP devices represent.
3. Weak default configurations remain a problem, as they do across a large class of consumer and enterprise products and software. The situation is likely to be much worse in the real world, considering the complexity of securely configuring a system with as many components as VoIP. Vendors must make an effort to provide secure-by-default configurations, and to educate users how best to protect their systems. Administrators are in need of tools to analyze their existing configurations for vulnerabilities. While some tools that dynamically test network components (e.g., firewalls), we need tools that work higher in the protocol and application stack (i.e., interacting at the user level). Furthermore, we need ways of validating configurations across multiple components and protocols.
4. Finally, there is simply no excuse for protocol-level vulnerabilities. While there exist techniques for analyzing and verifying security protocols, they do not seem to cope well with complexity. Aside from using such tools and continuing their development, protocol designers and standardization committees must consider the impact of their decisions on system implementers, i.e., whether it is likely

that a feature or aspect of the protocol is likely to be misunderstood and/or mis-
implemented. Simpler protocols are also desirable, but seem incompatible with
the trends we have observed in standardization bodies.

References

[1] 3GPP (2009) Generic Access Network. http://www.3gpp.org/ftp/Specs/html-info/43318.htm

[2] Abdelnur H, Cridlig V, State R, Festor O, Bourdellon J (2006) VoIP Security Assessment: Methods and Tools. In: Proceedings of the 1st IEEE Workshop on VoIP Management and Security (VoIP MASe), pp 29–34

[3] Abdelnur H, State R, Chrisment I, Popi C (2007) Assessing the security of VoIP Services. In: Proceedings of the 10th IFIP/IEEE Symposium on Integrated Management (IM), pp 373–382

[4] Abdelnur H, State R, Festor O (2007) KiF: A stateful SIP Fuzzer. In: Proceedings of the 1st International Conference on Principles, Systems and Applications of IP Telecommunications, pp 47–56

[5] Abdelnur H, Avanesov T, Rusinowitch M, State R (2008) Abusing SIP Authentication. In: Proceedings of the 4th International Conference on Information Assurance and Security (ISIAS), pp 237–242

[6] Abdelnur H, State R, Festor O (2008) Fuzzing for Vulnerabilities in the VoIP Space. In: Proceedings of the 17th Annual Conference of the European Institute for Computer Anti-Virus Research (EICAR)

[7] Ackermann R, Schumacher M, Roedig U, Steinmetz R (2001) Vulnerabilities and Security Limitations of current IP Telephony Systems. In: Proceedings of the Conference on Communications and Multimedia Security (CMS), pp 53–66

[8] Adelsbach A, Alkassar A, Garbe KH, Luzaic M, Manulis M, Scherer E, Schwenk J, Siemens E (2005) Voice over IP: Sichere Umstellung der Sprachkommunikation auf IP-Technologie. Bundesanzeiger Verlag

[9] Akbar MA, Farooq M (2009) Application of Evolutionary Algorithms in Detection of SIP based Flooding Attacks. In: Proceedings of the Genetic and Evolutionary Computation Conference (GECCO)

[10] Akbar MA, Farooq M (2010) RTP-Miner: A Real-time Security Framework for RTP Fuzzing Attacks. In: Proceedings of the 20th International Workshop on Network and Operating Systems Support for Digital Audio and Video (NOSSDAV)

[11] Akbar MA, Tariq Z, Farooq M (2008) A Comparative Study of Anomaly Detection Algorithms for Detection of SIP Flooding in IMS. In: Proceedings of the International Conference on Internet Multimedia Services Architecture and Applications (IMSAA)

[12] Al-Riyami S, Paterson K (2003) Certificateless Public Key Cryptography. In: Proceedings of AsiaCrypt, pp 452–473

[13] Albers J, Hahn B, McGann S, Park S, Zhu R (2005) An Analysis of Security Threats and Tools in SIP-Based VoIP Systems. M.Sc. Capstone Paper, Univesity of Colorado, Boulder

[14] Aleph One (1996) Smashing the stack for fun and profit. Phrack 7(49)

[15] Allain B (2005) VoIP Security Challenges and Approaches. In: Proceedings of the 2nd Workshop on Securing Voice over IP

[16] Anwar Z, Yurcik W, Johnson RE, Hafiz M, Campbell RH (2006) Multiple Design Patterns for Voice over IP (VoIP) Security. In: Proceedings of the IEEE Workshop on Information Assurance (WIA), held in conjunction with the 25th IEEE International Performance Computing and Communications Conference, (IPCCC)

[17] Apte V, Wu YS, Bagchi S, Garg S, Singh N (2006) SPACEDIVE: A Distributed Intrusion Detection System for Voice-over-IP Environments (Fast Abstract). In: Proceedings of the International Conference on Dependable Systems and Networks (DSN), pp 25–28

[18] Arkko J, Haverinen H (2006) Extensible Authentication Protocol Method for 3rd Generation Authentication and Key Agreement (EAP-AKA). RFC 4187 (Informational), URL http://www.ietf.org/rfc/rfc4187.txt

[19] Arkko J, Carrara E, Lindholm F, Naslund M, Norrman K (2004) MIKEY: Multimedia Internet KEYing. RFC 3830 (Proposed Standard), URL http://www.ietf.org/rfc/rfc3830.txt, updated by RFC 4738

[20] Aschenbruck N, Frank M, Martini P, Tolle J, Legat R, Richmann HD (2006) Present and Future Challenges Concerning DoS-attacks against PSAPs in VoIP Networks. In: Proceedings of the 4th IEEE International Workshop on Information Assurance (IWIA), pp 103–108

[21] Awais A, Farooq M, Javed MY (2008) Attack Analysis & Bio-inspired Security Framework for IP Multimedia Subsystem. In: Proceedings of the GECCO Conference Companion on Genetic and Evolutionary Computation, pp 2093–2098

[22] Balasubramaniyan V, Ahamad M, Park H (2007) CallRank: Combating SPIT Using Call Duration, Social Networks and Global Reputation. In: Proceedings of the 4th Conference on Email and Anti-Spam (CEAS)

[23] Banerjee N, Saklikar S, Saha S (2006) Anti-vamming Trust Enforcement in Peer-to-peer VoIP Networks. In: Proceedings of the International Conference on Communications and Mobile Computing (IWCMC), pp 201–206

[24] Barbieri R, Bruschi D, Rosti E (2002) Voice over IPsec: Analysis and Solutions. In: Proceedings of the 18th Annual Computer Security Applications Conference (ACSAC), pp 261–270

[25] Barry BIA, Anthony HA (2008) On the Performance of a Hybrid Intrusion Detection Architecture for Voice over IP Systems. In: Proceedings of the 4th International Conference on Security and Privacy in Communication Networks (SecureComm), pp 1–10

[26] Baset SA, Schulzrinne H (2006) An Analysis of the Skype Peer-to-Peer Telephony Protocol. In: Proceedings of INFOCOM

[27] Batchvarov A (2004) Security Issues and Solutions for Voice over IP Compared to Circuit Switched Networks. Tech. rep., INFOTECH Seminar Advanced Communication Services (ACS)

[28] Battistello P (2010) Work in Progress: Inter-Domain and DoS-Reistant Call Establishment Protocol (IDDR-CEP). In: Proceedings of the 4th Annual ACM Conference on Principles, Systems and Applications of IP Telecommunications (IPTCOMM), pp 25–34

[29] Baumann R, Cavin S, Schmid S (2006) Voice Over IP - Security and SPIT. KryptDet Report FU Br 41, Swiss Army

[30] Bellovin SM, Blaze M, Landau S (2005) The Real National-Security Needs for VoIP. Communications of the ACM (CACM) 48(11):120

[31] Berners-Lee T, Fielding R, Frystyk H (1996) Hypertext Transfer Protocol – HTTP/1.0. RFC 1945 (Informational), URL http://www.ietf.org/rfc/rfc1945.txt

[32] Berson T (2005) Skype Security Evaluation. Tech. rep.

[33] Bertrand M, Loudier Q, Gourhant Y, Bougant F, Osty M (2006) SPIT Mitigation by a Network-Level Anti-Spit Entity. In: Proceedings of the 3rd Workshop on Securing Voice over IP

[34] Bessis T, Rana A, Gurbani VK (2010) Session Initiation Protocol (SIP) Firewall for Internet Multimedia Subsystem (IMS) Core. Bell Labs Technical Journal

[35] Bilien J (2003) Key Agreement for Secure Voice over IP. Master of Science Thesis IMIT/LCN 2003-14, Royal Institute of Technology, Sweden

[36] Bilien J, Eliasson E, Vatn JO (2004) Call Establishment Delay for Secure VoIP. In: Proceedings of the Workshop on Modeling and Optimization in Mobile, Ad Hoc and Wireless Networks (WiOpt)

[37] Bilien J, Eliasson E, Orrblad J, Vatn JO (2005) Secure VoIP: Call Establishment and Media Protection. In: Proceedings of the 2nd Workshop on Securing Voice over IP

[38] Biondi P, Desclaux F (2006) Silver Needle in the Skype. In: Black-Hat Europe Conference, www.blackhat.com/presentations/bh-europe-06/bh-eu-06-biondi/bh-eu-06-biondi-up.pdf

[39] Bradbury D (2007) The Security Challenges Inherent in VoIP . Computers & Security 26(7–8):485–487

[40] Bremler-Barr A, Halachmi-Bekel R, Kangasharju K (2006) Unregister Attacks in SIP. In: Proceedings of the 2nd IEEE Workshop on Secure Network Protocols, pp 32–37

[41] Buschel A (2005) Authentication in VoIP. In: Proceedings of the 2nd Workshop on Securing Voice over IP

[42] Butcher D, Li X, Guo J (2007) Security Challenge and Defense in VoIP Infrastructures. IEEE Transactions on Systems, Man, and Cybernetics, Part C: Applications and Reviews 37(6):1152–1162

[43] Cao F, Jennings C (2006) Providing Response Identity and Authentication in IP Telephony. In: Proceedings of the 1st International Conference on Availability, Reliability and Security (ARES)

[44] Cao F, Malik S (2005) Security Analysis and Solutions for Deploying IP Telephony in the Critical Infrastructure. In: Proceedings of the workshop of the 1st International Conference on Security and Privacy for Emerging Areas in Communication Networks, pp 171–180

[45] Cao F, Malik S (2006) Vulnerability Analysis and Best Practices for Adopting IP Telephony in Critical Infrastructure Sectors. IEEE Communications Magazine 44(4):138–145

[46] Cao F, Ha B, Padmanabhan R, Yuan A, Tran K (2003) Call Filtering and Tracking in IP Telephony. In: Proceedings of the 7th IASTED International Conference on Internet and Multimedia Systems and Applications (IMSA)

[47] Casola V, Chianese R, Mazzeo A, Mazzocca N, Rak M (2004) A Policy-based Design Methodology and Performance Evaluation Framework for a Secure VoIP Infrastructure. In: Proceedings of the International Conference on E-business and TElecommunication Networks (ICETE)

[48] Casola V, Rak M, Mazzeo A, Mazzoccca N (2005) Security Design and Evaluation in a VoIP Secure Infrastructure: A Policy Based Approach. In: Proceedings of the International Conference on Information Technology: Coding and Computing, pp 727–732

[49] Chang CC, Lu YF, Pang AC, Kuo TW (2005) Design and Implementation of SIP Security. In: Proceedings of the International Conference On Information Networking (ICION), pp 669–678

[50] Chau J (2006) Security Issues Around the Deployment of VoIP and Multimedia Protocols in Wireless and Firewalled Environments. Computer Fraud & Security 2006(8):14–16

[51] Chen EY (2006) Detecting DoS Attacks on SIP Systems. In: Proceedings of the 1st IEEE Workshop on VoIP Management and Security (VoIP MaSe)

[52] Chen S, Wang X, Jajodia S (2006) On the Anonymity and Traceability of Peer-to-Peer VoIP Calls. IEEE Network 20(5):32–37

[53] Conner W, Nahrstedt K (2008) Protecting SIP Proxy Servers from Ringing-based Denial-of-Service Attacks. In: Proceedings of the 10th IEEE International Symposium on Multimedia (ISM), pp 340–347

[54] Cretu GF, Stavrou A, Locasto ME, Stolfo SJ, Keromytis AD (2008) Casting out Demons: Sanitizing Training Data for Anomaly Sensors. In: Proceedings of the IEEE Security and Privacy Symposium, pp 81–95

[55] Croft N, Olivier M (2005) A Model for Spam Prevention in Voice over IP Networks using Anonymous Verifying Authorities. In: Proceedings of the 5th Annual Information Security South Africa Conference (ISSA)

[56] Crosby SA, Wallach DS (2003) Denial of Service via Algorithmic Complexity Attacks. In: Proceedings of the 12th USENIX Security Symposium, pp 29–44

[57] cve-2003-1109 (2003) CVE-2003-1109. http://cve.mitre.org/cgi-bin/cvename.cgi?name=CVE-2003-1109

[58] Dagiuklas T, Geneiatakis D, Kambourakis G, Sisalem D, Ehlert S, Fiedler J, Markl J, Rokis M, Botron O, Rodriguez J, Liu J (2005) General Reliability and Security Framework for VoIP Infrastructures. Tech. Rep. Deliverable D2.2, SNOCER COOP-005892

[59] Dantu R, Kolan P (2004) Preventing Voice Spamming. In: Proceedings of the IEEE Global Telecommunications Conference (GLOBECOM), Workshop on VoIP Security Challenges and Solutions

[60] Dantu R, Kolan P (2005) Detecting Spam in VoIP Networks. In: Proceedings of the USENIX Workshop on Steps to Reducing Unwanted Traffic on the Internet (SRUTI), pp 31–37

[61] Dantu R, Fahmy S, Schulzrinne H, Cangussu J (2010) Issues and Challenges in Securing VoIP. Computers & Security (to appear)

[62] d'Heureuse N, Seedorf J, Niccolini S, Ewald T (2008) Protecting SIP-Based Networks and Services from Unwanted Communications. In: Proceedings of the IEEE Global Telecommunications Conference (GLOBECOM), pp 1–5

[63] d'Heureuse N, Seedorf J, Niccolini S (2009) A Policy Framework for Personalized and Role-Based SPIT Prevention. In: Proceedings of the 3rd International Conference on Principles, Systems and Applications of IP Telecommunications (IPTCOMM)

[64] Dierks T, Rescorla E (2008) The Transport Layer Security (TLS) Protocol Version 1.2. RFC 5246 (Proposed Standard), URL http://www.ietf.org/rfc/rfc5246.txt

[65] Ding Y, Su G (2007) Intrusion Detection System for Signal-based SIP Attacks Through Timed HCPN. In: Proceedings of the 2nd International Conference on Availability, Reliability and Security (ARES), pp 190–197

[66] Dritsas S, Mallios J, Theoharidou M, Marias GF, Gritzalis D (2007) Threat Analysis of the Session Initiation Protocol Regarding Spam. In: Proceedings of the 26th IEEE International Performance Computing and Communications Conference (IPCCC), pp 426–433

[67] Dritsas S, Soupionis Y, Theoharidou M, Mallios Y, Gritzalis D (2008) SPIT Identification Criteria Implementation: Effectiveness and Lessons Learned. In: Proceedings of the 23rd IFIP TC11 International Information Security Conference (SEC), pp 381–395

[68] Dritsas S, Dritsou V, Tsoumas B, Constantopoulos P, Gritzalis D (2009) OntoSPIT: SPIT management through ontologies. Computer Communications 32(1):203–212

[69] Droms R (1997) Dynamic Host Configuration Protocol. RFC 2131 (Draft Standard), URL http://www.ietf.org/rfc/rfc2131.txt, updated by RFCs 3396, 4361, 5494

[70] Durlanik A, Sogukpinar I (2005) SIP Authentication Scheme Using ECDH. World Academy Science, Engineering and Technology (WASET) 8:350–353

[71] Dwivedi H (2008) Hacking VoIP. O'Reilly

[72] Edelson E (2005) Voice over IP: Security Pitfalls. Network Security 2005(2):4–7

[73] Ehlert S, Wang C, Magedanz T, Sisalem D (2008) Specification-based Denial-of-Service Detection for SIP Voice-over-IP Networks. In: Proceedings of the 3rd International Conference on Internet Monitoring and Protection, pp 59–66

[74] Ehlert S, Zhang G, Geneiatakis D, Kambourakis G, Dagiuklas T, Markl J, Sisalem D (2008) Two Layer Denial of Service Prevention on SIP VoIP Infrastructures. Computer Communications 31(10):2443–2456

[75] Ehlert S, Zhang G, Magedanz T (2008) Increasing SIP Firewall Performance by Ruleset Size Limitation. In: Proceedings of the 19th IEEE International Symposium on Personal, Indoor and Mobile Radio Communications (PIMRC), pp 1–6

[76] Ehlert S, Rebahi Y, Magedanz T (2009) Intrusion Detection System for Denial-of-Service Flooding Attacks in SIP Communication Networks. International Journal of Security and Networks 4(3):189–200

[77] Elbayoumy AD, Shepherd S (2005) A High Grade Secure VoIP System Using an Endpoint CPU Capability Detector. In: Proceedings of the ITA05 International Conference on Internet Technologies and Applications, pp 173–180

[78] Elbayoumy AD, Shepherd S (2005) A High Grade Secure VoIP System Using the Tiny Encryption Algorithm. In: Proceedings of the 7th Annual International Symposium on Advanced Radio Technologies, pp 342–350

[79] Elbayoumy AD, Shepherd S (2005) QoS Control Using an Endpoint CPU Capability Detector in a Secure VoIP System. In: Proceedings of the 10th IEEE Symposium on Computers and Communications, pp 175–181

[80] Elbayoumy AD, Shepherd S (2007) A Comprehensive Secure VoIP Solution. International Journal of Network Security 5(2):233–240

[81] Elbayoumy AD, Shepherd S (2007) Stream or Block Cipher for Securing VoIP? International Journal of Network Security 5(2):128–133

[82] Eun-Chul C, Hyoung-Kee C, Sung-Jae C (2007) Evaluation of Security Protocols for the Session Initiation Protocol. In: Proceedings of the 16th International Conference on Computer Communications and Networks (ICCCN), pp 611–616

[83] Fessi A, Evans N, Niedermayer H, Holz R (2010) Pr2-P2PSIP: Privacy Preserving P2P Signaling for VoIP and IM. In: Proceedings of the 4th Annual ACM Conference on Principles, Systems and Applications of IP Telecommunications (IPTCOMM), pp 141–152

[84] Fiedler J, Kupka T, Ehlert S, Magedanz T, Sisalem D (2007) VoIP Defender: Highly Scalable SIP-based Security Architecture. In: Proceedings of the 1st International Conference on Principles, Systems and Applications of IP Telecommunications (IPTComm), pp 11–17

[85] Fielding R, Gettys J, Mogul J, Frystyk H, Masinter L, Leach P, Berners-Lee T (1999) Hypertext Transfer Protocol – HTTP/1.1. RFC 2616 (Draft Standard), URL http://www.ietf.org/rfc/rfc2616.txt, updated by RFC 2817

[86] Finlayson R (1984) Bootstrap loading using TFTP. RFC 906, URL http://www.ietf.org/rfc/rfc906.txt

[87] Floroiu J, Sisalem D (2009) A Comparative Analysis of the Security Aspects of the Multimedia Key Exchange Protocols. In: Proceedings of the 3rd International Conference on Principles, Systems and Applications of IP Telecommunications (IPTComm), pp 2:1–2:10

[88] Franks J, Hallam-Baker P, Hostetler J, Lawrence S, Leach P, Luotonen A, Stewart L (1999) HTTP Authentication: Basic and Digest Access Authentication. RFC 2617 (Draft Standard), URL http://www.ietf.org/rfc/rfc2617.txt

[89] Fuchs C, Aschenbruck N, Leder F, Martini P (2008) Detecting VoIP-based DoS Attacks at the Public Safety Answering Point. In: Proceedings of the ACM Aymposium on Information, Computer and Communications Security (ASIACCS), pp 148–155

[90] Geneiatakis D, Keromytis AD (2011) Towards a Forensic Analysis for Multimedia Communication Services. In: Proceedings of the 7th International Symposium on Frontiers in Networking with Applications (FINA)

[91] Geneiatakis D, Lambrinoudakis C (2007) A Lightweight Protection Mechanism against Signaling Attacks in a SIP-based VoIP Environment. Telecommunication Systems 36(4):153–159

[92] Geneiatakis D, Lambrinoudakis C (2007) An Ontology Description for SIP Security Flaws. Computer Communications 30(6):1367–1374

[93] Geneiatakis D, Lambrinoudakis C (2008) A Cost-Effective Mechanism for Protecting SIP Based Internet Telephony Services Against Signaling Attacks. In: Proceedings of the IMS and Mobile Multimedia Workshop

[94] Geneiatakis D, Kambourakis G, Dagiuklas T, Lambrinoudakis C, Gritzalis S (2005) SIP Security Mechanisms: A state-of-the-art review. In: Proceedings of the 5th International Network Conference (INC)

[95] Geneiatakis D, Kambourakis G, Dagiuklas T, Lambrinoudakis C, Gritzalis S (2005) A Framework for Detecting Malformed Messages in SIP Networks. In: Proceedings of 14th IEEE Workshop on Local and Metropolitan Area Networks (LANMAN)

[96] Geneiatakis D, Kambourakis G, Lambrinoudakis C, Dagiuklas T, Gritzalis S (2005) SIP Message Tampering: THE SQL code INJECTION attack. In: Proceedings of 13th IEEE International Conference on Software, Telecommunications and Computer Networks (SoftCOM)

[97] Geneiatakis D, Dagiuklas T, Kambourakis G, Lambrinoudakis C, Gritzalis S, Ehlert KS, Sisalem D (2006) Survey of Security Vulnerabilities in Session Initiation Protocol. IEEE Communications Surveys & Tutorials 8(3):68–81

[98] Geneiatakis D, Dagiuklas T, Lambrinoudakis C, Kambourakis G, Gritzalis S (2006) Novel Protecting Mechanism for SIP-based Infrastructure against

Malformed Message Attacks: Performance Evaluation Study. In: Proceedings of the 5th International Conference on Communication Systems, Networks and Digital Signal Processing (CSNDSP), pp 261–266

[99] Geneiatakis D, Kambourakis G, Dagiuklas T, Lambrinoudakis C, Gritzalis S (2007) A Framework for Detecting Malformed Messages in SIP Networks. Computer Networks: The International Journal of Computer and Telecommunications Networking 51(10):2580–2593

[100] Geneiatakis D, Kambourakis G, Lambrinoudakis C, Dagiouklas A, Gritzalis S (2007) A Framework for Protecting SIP-based Infrastructure against Malformed Message Attacks. Computer Networks 51(10):2580–2593

[101] Geneiatakis D, Kambourakis G, Lambrinoudakis C (2008) A Mechanism for Ensuring the Validity and Accuracy of the Billing Services in IP Telephony. In: Proceedings of the 5th International Conference on Trust, Privacy & Security in Digital Business (TrustBus), pp 59–68

[102] Geneiatakis D, Lambrinoudakis C, Kambourakis G (2008) An Ontology Based Policy for Deploying Secure SIP-based VoIP Services. Computers and Security 27(7–8):285–297

[103] Geneiatakis D, Vrakas N, Lambrinoudakis C (2009) Performance Evaluation of a Flooding Detection Mechanism for VoIP Networks. In: Proceedings of the 16th International Workshop on Systems Signals and Image Processing, pp 1–5

[104] Geneiatakis D, Vrakas N, Lambrinoudakis C (2009) Utilizing Bloom Filters for Detecting Flooding Attacks against SIP Based Services. Computers and Security 28(7):578–591

[105] Gritzalis D, Mallios Y (2008) A SIP-oriented SPIT Management Framework. Computers & Security 27(5–6):136–153

[106] Guang-Yu H, Wen WYY, Zhao H (2008) SPIT Detection and Prevention Method Based on Signal Analysis. In: Proceedings of the 3rd International Conference on Convergence and Hybrid Information Technology (ICCIT), vol 2, pp 631–638

[107] Guo JI, Yen JC, Pai HF (2002) New Voice over Internet Protocol Technique with Hierarchical Data Security Protection. IEE Proceedings — Vision, Image and Signal Processing 149(4):237–243

[108] Gupta P, Shmatikov V (2007) Security Analysis of Voice-over-IP Protocols. In: Proceedings of the 20th IEEE Computer Security Foundations Symposium (CSFW), pp 49–63

[109] Gurbani VK, Kolesnikov V (2010) Work in Progress: A secure and lightweight scheme for media keying in the Session Initiation Protocol (SIP). In: Proceedings of the 4th Annual ACM Conference on Principles, Systems and Applications of IP Telecommunications (IPTCOMM), pp 35–44

[110] Gurbani VK, Kolesnikov V (2011) A Survey and Analysis of Media Keying Techniques in the Session Initiation Protocol (SIP). IEEE Communications Surveys and Tutorials (to appear)

[111] Gurbani VK, Willis D, Audet F (2007) Cryptographically Transparent Session Initiation Protocol (SIP) Proxies. In: Proceedings of the IEEE International Conference on Communications (ICC), pp 1185–1190

[112] Haberler M, Lendl O (2006) Secure Selective Peering with Federations. In: Proceedings of the 3rd Workshop on Securing Voice over IP

[113] Handley M, Jacobson V, Perkins C (2006) SDP: Session Description Protocol. RFC 4566 (Proposed Standard), URL http://www.ietf.org/rfc/rfc4566.txt

[114] Handley M, Rescorla E, IAB (2006) Internet Denial-of-Service Considerations. RFC 4732 (Informational), URL http://www.ietf.org/rfc/rfc4732.txt

[115] Hansen M, Hansen M, Möller J, Rohwer T, Tolkmit C, Waack H (2006) Developing a Legally Compliant Reachability Management System as a Countermeasure against SPIT. In: Proceedings of the 3rd Workshop on Securing Voice over IP

[116] Hansen P, Woodward A (2007) Network Security—Is IP Telephony Helping The Cause? In: Proceedings of the 5th Australian Information Security Management Conference, pp 73–79

[117] Hantehzadeh N, Mehta A, Gurbani VK, Gupta L, Ho TK, Wilathgamuwa G (2011) Statistical analysis of self-similar Session Initiation Protocol (SIP) messages for anomaly detection. In: Proceedings of the 4th IFIP/IEEE International Conference on New Technologies, Mobility, and Security (NTMS)

[118] Harkins D, Carrel D (1998) The Internet Key Exchange (IKE). RFC 2409 (Proposed Standard), URL http://www.ietf.org/rfc/rfc2409.txt, obsoleted by RFC 4306, updated by RFC 4109

[119] Harrington D, Presuhn R, Wijnen B (2002) An Architecture for Describing Simple Network Management Protocol (SNMP) Management Frameworks. RFC 3411 (Standard), URL http://www.ietf.org/rfc/rfc3411.txt, updated by RFC 5343

[120] Haverinen H, Salowey J (2006) Extensible Authentication Protocol Method for Global System for Mobile Communications (GSM) Subscriber Identity Modules (EAP-SIM). RFC 4186 (Informational), URL http://www.ietf.org/rfc/rfc4186.txt

[121] Hlavacs H, Gansterer WN, Schabauer H, Zottl J, Petraschek M, Hoeher T, Jung O (2008) Enhancing ZRTP by using Computational Puzzles. Journal of Universal Compter Science 14(5):693–716

[122] Huang HF, Wei WC (2006) A New Efficient Authentication Scheme for Session Initiation Protocol. In: Proceedings of the Joint Conference on Information Sciences (JCIS), 9th International Conference on Computer Science and Informatics

[123] Hung PCK, Martin MV (2006) Security Issues in VoIP Applications. In: Proceedings of the Canadian Conference on Electrical and Computer Engineering (CCECE), pp 2361–2364

[124] Hung PCK, Martin MV (2006) Through the looking glass: Security issues in VoIP applications. In: Proceedings of the IADIS International Conference on Applied Computing

[125] Hunter P (2002) VOIP the Latest Security Concern: DoS Attack the Greatest Threat. Network Security 2002(11):5–7

[126] Hyun-Soo C, Jea-Tek R, Byeong-hee R, Jeong-Wook K, Hyun-Cheol J (2008) Detection of SIP De-Registration and Call-Disruption Attacks Using a Retransmission Mechanism and a Countermeasure Scheme. In: Proceedings of the IEEE International Conference on Signal Image Technology and Internet Based Systems (SITIS), pp 650–656

[127] Hyung-Jong K, Joo KM, Yoonjeong K, Cheol JH (2009) DEVS-based Modeling of VoIP Spam Callers' Behavior for SPIT Level Calculation. Simulation Modeling Practice and Theory 17(4):569–584

[128] Insu K, Keecheon K (2007) Secure Session Management Mechanism in VoIP Service. In: Proceedings of the Workshop on Ubiquitous Processing for Wireless Networks (UPWN), held in conjunction with the 5th International Symposium on Parallel and Distributed Processing and Applications (ISPA), pp 96–104

[129] James P, Woodward A (2007) Securing VoIP: A Framework to Mitigate or Manage Risks. In: Proceedings of the 5th Australian Information Security Management Conference, pp 103–116

[130] Janne JL, Komu M (2007) Cure for Spam Over Internet Telephony. In: Proceedings of the 4th IEEE Consumer Communications and Networking Conference (CCNC), pp 896–900

[131] Johansson I, Westerlund M (2009) Support for Reduced-Size Real-Time Transport Control Protocol (RTCP): Opportunities and Consequences. RFC 5506 (Proposed Standard), URL http://www.ietf.org/rfc/rfc5506.txt

[132] Kaksonen R, Laakso M, Takanen A (????) Software Security Assessment through Specification Mutations and Fault Injection

[133] Kaufman C (2005) Internet Key Exchange (IKEv2) Protocol. RFC 4306 (Proposed Standard), URL http://www.ietf.org/rfc/rfc4306.txt, updated by RFC 5282

[134] Kent S (2005) IP Encapsulating Security Payload (ESP). RFC 4303 (Proposed Standard), URL http://www.ietf.org/rfc/rfc4303.txt

[135] Kent S, Seo K (2005) Security Architecture for the Internet Protocol. RFC 4301 (Proposed Standard), URL http://www.ietf.org/rfc/rfc4301.txt

[136] Keromytis AD (2009) Voice over IP: Risks, Threats and Vulnerabilities. In: Proceedings of the Cyber Infrastructure Protection (CIP) Conference

[137] Keromytis AD (2010) A Look at VoIP Vulnerabilities. USENIX ;login: Magazine 35(1):41–50

[138] Keromytis AD (2010) Voice over IP Security: Research and Practice. IEEE Security & Privacy Magazine 8(2):76–78

[139] Kolan P, Dantu R (2007) Socio-technical Defense Against Voice Spamming. ACM Transactions on Autonomous and Adaptive Systems (TAAS) 2(1)

[140] Kolan P, Dantu R, Cangussu JW (2008) Nuisance of a Voice Call. ACM Transactions on Multimedia Computing, Communications and Applications (TOMCCAP) 5(1):6:1–6:22

[141] Kong L, Balasubramaniyan VB, Ahamad M (2006) A Lightweight Scheme for Securely and Reliably Locating SIP Users. In: Proceedings of the 1st IEEE Workshop on VoIP Management and Security (VoIP MaSe), pp 9–17

[142] Kotulski Z, Mazurczyk W (2006) Covert Channel for Improving VoIP Security. In: Proceedings of the 13th International Multi-Conference on Advanced Computer Systems (ACS), pp 311–320

[143] Krebs B (2009) Security Fix: Default Passwords Led to $55 Million in Bogus Phone Charges. URL http://voices.washingtonpost.com/securityfix/2009/06/default_passwords_led_to_55_mi.html

[144] Kuhn DR, Walsh TJ, Fries S (2005) Security Considerations for Voice Over IP Systems. US National Institute of Standards and Technology (NIST) Special Publication SP 800-58

[145] Kuntze N, Schmidt AU, Hett C (2007) Non-Repudiation in Internet Telephony. In: Proceedings of the IFIP International Information Security Conference, pp 361–372

[146] Kurmus A, Garet JF (2009) Studying and Experimenting with Threats Against Voice over IP Systems. Tech. Rep. Masters Thesis, EURECOM

[147] Kuthan J (2001) Internet Telephony Traversal Across Decomposed Firewalls and NATs. In: Proceedings of the 2nd IP Telephony Workshop

[148] Lakay ET, Agbinya JI (2005) Security Issues in SIP Signaling in Wireless Networks and Services. In: Proceedings of the International Conference on Mobile Business, pp 639–642

[149] Larson J, Dawson T, Evans M, Straley JC (2004) Defending VoIP Networks from Distributed DoS (DDoS) Attacks. In: Proceedings of the IEEE Global Telecommunications Conference (GLOBECOM)

[150] Larson J, Dawson T, Evans M, Straley JC (2005) Defending VoIP Networks from DDoS Attacks. In: Proceedings of the 2nd Workshop on Securing Voice over IP

[151] Lee CC (2009) On Security of An Efficient Nonce-based Authentication Scheme for SIP. International Journal of Network Security 9(3):201–203

[152] Li C, Li S, Zhang D, Chen G (2006) Cryptanalysis of a Data Security Protection Scheme for VoIP. IEE Proceedings—Vision, Image and Signal Processing 153(1):1–10

[153] Luo M, Peng T, Leckie C (2008) CPU-based DoS Attacks Against SIP Servers. In: Proceedings of the IEEE Network Operations and Management Symposium (NOMS), pp 41–48

[154] MacIntosh R, Vinokurov D (2005) Detection and Mitigation of Spam in IP Telephony Networks Using Signaling Protocol Analysis. In: Proceedings of

the IEEE/Sarnoff Symposium on Advances in Wired and Wireless Communication, pp 49–52

[155] Madhosingh A (2006) The Design of a Differentiated SIP to Control VoIP Spam. Masters Thesis Report SPIT, CAPTCHA, Florida State University, Computer Science Department

[156] Mandjes M, Saniee I, Stolyar AL (2001) Load characterization and Anomaly Detection for Voice over IP Traffic (Extended Abstract). In: Proceedings of the ACM SIGMETRICS Conference

[157] Mandjes M, Saniee I, A L Stolyar A (2005) Load Characterization and Anomaly Detection for Voice over IP Traffic. IEEE Transactions on Neural Networks 16(5):1019–1026

[158] Marias GF, Dritsas S, Theoharidou M, Mallios J, Gritzalis D (2007) SIP Vulnerabilities and Anti-SPIT Mechanisms Assessment. In: Proceedings of the 16th International Conference on Computer Communications and Networks (ICCCN), pp 597–604

[159] Marias GF, Dritsas S, Theoharidou M, Mallios J, Mitrou L, Gritzalis D, Dagiuklas T, Rebahi Y, Ehlert S, Pannier B, Capsada O, Juell JF (2007) SPIT Detection and Handling Strategies for VoIP Infrastructures. Tech. Rep. Deliverable WP2/D2.2, SPIDER COOP-32720

[160] Marshall W, Faryar AF, Kealy K, de los Reyes G, Rosencrantz I, Rosencrantz R, Spielman C (2006) Carrier VoIP Security Architecture. In: Proceedings of the 12th International Telecommunications Network Strategy and Planning Symposium, pp 1–6

[161] Martin MV, Hung PCK (2005) Towards a Security Policy for VoIP Applications. In: Proceedings of the Canadian Conference on Electrical and Computer Engineering (CCECE), pp 65–68

[162] Mathieu B, Niccolini S, Sisalem D (2008) SDRS: A Voice-over-IP Spam Detection and Reaction System. IEEE Security & Privacy Magazine 6(6):52–59

[163] Mazurczyk W, Kotulski Z (2005) New Security and Control Protocol for VoIP Based on Steganography and Digital Watermarking. Technical report, Institute of Fundamental Technological Research, Polish Academy of Sciences

[164] Mazurczyk W, Kotulski Z (2006) New VoIP Traffic Security Scheme with Digital Watermarking. In: Proceedings of International Conference on Computer Safety, Reliability, and Security (SafeComp), pp 170–181

[165] McGann S, Sicker D (2005) An Analysis of Security Threats and Tools in SIP-Based VoIP Systems. In: Proceedings of the 2nd VoIP Security Workshop

[166] Me G, Verdone D (2006) An Overview of Some Techniques to Exploit VoIP over WLAN. In: Proceedings of the International Conference on Digital Telecommunications (ICDT), pp 67–73

[167] Mehta A, Hantehzadeh N, Gurbani VK, Ho TK, Koshiko J, Vishwanathan R (2011) On the inefficacy of Euclidean classifiers for detecting self-similar Session Initiation Protocol (SIP) messages. In: Proceedings of the 12th IFIP/IEEE International Symposium on Integrated Network Management (IM)

[168] Melchor CA, Deswarte Y, Iguchi-Cartigny J (2007) Closed-circuit Unobservable Voice over IP. In: Proceedings of the 23rd Annual Computer Security Applications Conference (ACSAC), pp 119–128

[169] Mills D (1992) Network Time Protocol (Version 3) Specification, Implementation and Analysis. RFC 1305 (Draft Standard), URL http://www.ietf.org/rfc/rfc1305.txt

[170] Mockapetris P (1987) Domain names - concepts and facilities. RFC 1034 (Standard), URL http://www.ietf.org/rfc/rfc1034.txt, updated by RFCs 1101, 1183, 1348, 1876, 1982, 2065, 2181, 2308, 2535, 4033, 4034, 4035, 4343, 4035, 4592

[171] Mockapetris P (1987) Domain names - implementation and specification. RFC 1035 (Standard), URL http://www.ietf.org/rfc/rfc1035.txt, updated by RFCs 1101, 1183, 1348, 1876, 1982, 1995, 1996, 2065, 2136, 2181, 2137, 2308, 2535, 2845, 3425, 3658, 4033, 4034, 4035, 4343

[172] Modadugu N, Rescorla E (2004) The Design and Implementation of Datagram TLS. In: Proceedings of the ISOC Symposium on Network and Distributed Systems Security (NDSS)

[173] Mohammadi-nodooshan A, Darmani Y, Jalili R, Nourani M (2008) A Robust and Efficient SIP Authentication Scheme. In: Proceedings of the 13th International CSI Computer Conference (CSICC), pp 551–558

[174] Nassar M, Niccolini S, State R, Ewald T (2007) Holistic VoIP Intrusion Detection and Prevention System. In: Proceedings of the 1st International Conference on Principles, Systems and Applications of IP Telecommunications (IPTCOMM), pp 1–9

[175] Nassar M, State R, Festor O (2007) VoIP Honeypot Architecture. In: Proceedings of the 10th IFIP/IEEE International Symposium on Integrated Network Management, pp 109–118

[176] Nassar M, State R, Festor O (2008) Monitoring SIP Traffic Using Support Vector Machines. In: Proceedings of the Symposium on Recent Advances in Intrusion Detection (RAID), pp 311–330

[177] Niccolini S (2006) SPIT Prevention: State of the Art and Research Challenges. In: Proceedings of the 3rd Workshop on Securing Voice over IP

[178] Niccolini S, Garroppo RG, Giordano S, Risi G, Ventura S (2006) SIP Intrusion Detection and Prevention: Recommendations and Prototype Implementation. In: Proceedings of the 1st IEEE Workshop on VoIP Management and Security (VoIP MaSe), pp 47–52

[179] Ong L, Yoakum J (2002) An Introduction to the Stream Control Transmission Protocol (SCTP). RFC 3286 (Informational), URL http://www.ietf.org/rfc/rfc3286.txt

[180] Ono K, Schulzrinne H (2009) Have I Met You Before? Using Cross-Media Relations to Reduce SPIT. In: Proceedings of the 3rd International Conference on Principles, Systems and Applications of IP Telecommunications (IPTComm), pp 1–7

[181] Ormazabal G, Nagpal S, Yardeni E, Schulzrinne H (2008) Secure SIP: A Scalable Prevention Mechanism for DoS Attacks on SIP Based VoIP Sys-

tems. In: Proceedings of the 2nd International Conference on Principles, Systems and Applications of IP Telecommunications (IPTComm), pp 107–132

[182] Palmieri F, Fiore U (2009) Providing True End-to-End Security in Converged Voice over IP Infrastructures. Computers & Security 28(6):433–449

[183] Patankar P, Nam G, Kesidis G, Das CR (2008) Exploring Anti-Spam Models in Large Scale VoIP Systems. In: Proceedings of the 28th International Conference on Distributed Computing Systems (ICDCS), pp 85–92

[184] Persky D (2007) VoIP Security Vulnerabilities. White paper, SANS Institute

[185] Petraschek M, Hoeher T, Jung O, Hlavacs H, Gansterer WN (2008) Security and Usability Aspects of Man-in-the-Middle Attacks on ZRTP. Journal of Universal Computer Science 14(5):673–692

[186] Phithakkitnukoon S, Dantu R (2009) Defense Against SPIT Using Community Signals. In: Proceedings of the IEEE International Conference on Intelligence and Security Informatics (ISI)

[187] Pörschmann C, Knospe H (2008) Analysis of Spectral Parameters of Audio Signals for the Identification of Spam Over IP Telephony. In: Proceedings of the 5th Conference on Email and Anti-Spam (CEAS)

[188] Posegga J, Seedorf J (2005) Voice Over IP: Unsafe at any Bandwidth? In: Proceedings of the Eurescom Summit: Ubiquitous Services and Applications Exploiting the Potential

[189] Postel J (1980) User Datagram Protocol. RFC 768 (Standard), URL http://www.ietf.org/rfc/rfc768.txt

[190] Postel J (1981) Transmission Control Protocol. RFC 793 (Standard), URL http://www.ietf.org/rfc/rfc793.txt, updated by RFCs 1122, 3168

[191] Quinten VM, van de Meent R, Pras A (2007) Analysis of Techniques for Protection Against Spam over Internet Telephony. In: Proceedings of the 13th Open European Summer School and IFIP TC6.6 Workshop (EUNICE), pp 70–77

[192] Quittek J, Niccolini S, Tartarelli S, Schlegel R (2006) Prevention of Spam over IP Telephony (SPIT). NEC Technical Journal 1(2):114–119

[193] Quittek J, Niccolini S, Tartarelli S, Stiemerling M, Brunner M, Ewald T (2007) Detecting SPIT Calls by Checking Human Communication Patterns. In: Proceedings of the IEEE International Conference on Communications (ICC), pp 1979–1984

[194] Quittek J, Niccolini S, Tartarelli S, Schlegel R (2008) On Spam over Internet Telephony (SPIT) Prevention. IEEE Communications Magazine 46(8):80–86

[195] Rafique MZ, Akbar MA, Farooq M (2009) Evaluating DoS Attacks Against SIP-Based VoIP Systems. In: Proceedings of the IEEE Global Telecommunications Conference (GLOBECOM)

[196] Ramsdell B (2004) Secure/Multipurpose Internet Mail Extensions (S/MIME) Version 3.1 Message Specification. RFC 3851 (Proposed Standard), URL http://www.ietf.org/rfc/rfc3851.txt

[197] Ranganathan MK, Kilmartin L (2003) Performance Analysis of Secure Session Initiation Protocol Based VoIP Networks. Computer Communications 26(6):552–565

[198] Reason J, Messerschmitt D (2001) The Impact of Confidentiality on Quality of Service in Heterogeneous Voice over IP Networks. In: Proceedings of the IEEE Conference on Management of Multimedia Networks and Services, pp 175–192

[199] Rebahi Y, Sisalem D (2005) SIP Service Providers and the Spam Problem. In: Proceedings of the 2nd VoIP Security Workshop

[200] Rebahi Y, Sisalem D, Magedanz T (2006) SIP Spam Detection. In: Proceedings of the International Conference on Digital Telecommunications(ICDT), pp 29–31

[201] Rebahi Y, Ehlert S, Dritsas S, Marias GF, Gritzalis D, Pannier B, Capsada O, Golubenco T, Juell JF, Hoffmann M (2007) General Anti-Spam Security Framework for VoIP Infrastructures. Tech. Rep. Deliverable WP2/D2.3, SPIDER COOP-32720

[202] Rebahi Y, Ehlert S, Theoharidou M, Mallios J, Dritsas S, Marias GF, Mitrou L, Dagiuklas T, Avgoustianakis M, Gritzalis D, Pannier B, Capsada O, Markl J (2007) SPIT Threat Analysis. Deliverable wp2/d2.1, SPIDER COOP-32720

[203] Rebahi Y, Pallares JJ, Kovacs G, Minh NT, Ehlert S, Sisalem D (2008) Performance Analysis of Identity Management in the Session Initiation Protocol (SIP). In: Proceedings of the IEEE/ACS International Conference on Computer Systems and Applications (AICCSA), pp 711–717

[204] Rebahi Y, Sher M, Magedanz T (2008) Detecting Flooding Attacks Against IP Multimedia Subsystem (IMS) Networks. In: Proceedings of the IEEE/ACS International Conference on Computer Systems and Applications, pp 848–851

[205] Rescorla E, Modadugu N (2006) Datagram Transport Layer Security. RFC 4347 (Proposed Standard), URL http://www.ietf.org/rfc/rfc4347.txt

[206] Reynolds B, Ghosal D (2002) STEM: Secure Telephony Enabled Middlebox. IEEE Communications Magazine 40(10):52–58

[207] Reynolds B, Ghosal D (2003) Secure IP Telephony using Multi-layered Protection. In: Proceedings of the ISOC Symposium on Network and Distributed Systems Security (NDSS)

[208] Rieck K, Wahl S, Laskov P, Domschitz P, Müller KR (2008) A Self-learning System for Detection of Anomalous SIP Messages. In: Proceedings of the 2nd Internation Conference on Principles, Systems and Applications of IP Telecommunications. Services and Security for Next Generation Networks: Second International Conference, (IPTComm), pp 90–106

[209] Ring J, Choo KKR, Foo E, Looi M (2006) A New authentication Mechanism and Key Agreement Protocol for SIP Using Identity-based Cryptography. In: Proceedings of AusCERT, R&D Stream, pp 61–72

[210] Rippon WJ (2006) Threat Assessment of IP Based Voice Systems. In: Proceedings of the 1st IEEE Workshop on VoIP Management and Security (VoIP MaSe), pp 19–28

[211] Roedig U, Ackermann R, Steinmetz R (2000) Evaluating and Improving Firewalls for IP-Telephony Environments. In: Proceedings of the 1st IP Telephony Workshop

[212] Rosenberg J, Schulzrinne H, Camarillo G, Johnston A, Peterson J, Sparks R, Handley M, Schooler E (2002) SIP: Session Initiation Protocol. RFC 3261 (Proposed Standard), URL http://www.ietf.org/rfc/rfc3261.txt, updated by RFCs 3265, 3853, 4320, 4916, 5393

[213] Rosenberg J, Mahy R, Matthews P, Wing D (2008) Session Traversal Utilities for NAT (STUN). RFC 5389 (Proposed Standard), URL http://www.ietf.org/rfc/rfc5389.txt

[214] Saklikar S, Saha S (2007) Identity Federation for VoIP-based Services. In: Proceedings of the ACM Workshop on Digital Identity Management, pp 62–71

[215] Salsano S, Veltri L, Papalilo D (2002) SIP Security Issues: The SIP Authentication Procedure and its Processing Load. IEEE Network 16(6):38–44

[216] Schlegel R, Niccolini S, Tartarelli S, Brunner M (2006) SPam over Internet Telephony (SPIT) Prevention Framework. In: Proceedings of the IEEE Global Telecommunications Conference (GLOBECOM), pp 1–6

[217] Schmidt H, Dang CT, Hauck FJ (2007) Proxy-based Security for the Session Initiation Protocol(SIP). In: Proceedings of the 2nd International Conference on Systems and Networks Communications (ICSNC), pp 42–47

[218] Scholz H (2006) Attacking VoIP Networks. In: Proceedings of the 3rd Workshop on Securing Voice over IP

[219] Schulzrinne H, Casner S, Frederick R, Jacobson V (2003) RTP: A Transport Protocol for Real-Time Applications. RFC 3550 (Standard), URL http://www.ietf.org/rfc/rfc3550.txt, updated by RFC 5506

[220] Seedorf J (2006) Security challenges for peer-to-peer SIP. IEEE Network 20(5):38–45

[221] Seedorf J (2006) Using Cryptographically Generated SIP-URIs to Protect the Integrity of Content in P2P-SIP. In: Proceedings of the 3rd Workshop on Securing Voice over IP

[222] Sengar H, Dantu R, Wijesekera D (2005) Securing VoIP and PSTN from Integrated Signaling Network Vulnerabilities. In: Proceedings of the 1st IEEE Workshop on VoIP Management and Security, pp 1–7

[223] Sengar H, Wijesekera D, Jajodia S, Dantu R (2005) Securing VoIP from Signaling Network Vulnerabilities. In: Proceedings of the 2nd Workshop on Securing Voice over IP

[224] Sengar H, Wang H, Wijesekera D, Jajodia S (2006) Fast Detection of Denial-of-Service Attacks on IP Telephony. In: Proceedings of the 14th IEEE International Workshop on Quality of Service (IWQoS), pp 199–208

[225] Sengar H, Wijesekera D, Wang H, Jajodia S (2006) VoIP Intrusion Detection Through Interacting Protocol State Machines. In: Proceedings of the International Conference on Dependable Systems and Networks (DSN), pp 393–402

[226] Sengar H, Wang H, Wijesekera D, Jajodia S (2008) Detecting VoIP Floods Using the Hellinger Distance. IEEE Transactions on Parallel and Distributed Systems 19(6):794–805

[227] Seo D, Lee H, Nuwere E (2008) Detecting More SIP Attacks on VoIP Services by Combining Rule Matching and State Transition Models. In: Proceedings of the 23rd IFIP TC11 International Information Security Conference (SEC), pp 397–411

[228] Shah G, Molina A, Blaze M (2006) Keyboards and Covert Channels. In: Proceedings of 15th USENIX Security Symposium, pp 59–75

[229] Shen C, Nahum E, Schulzrinne H, Wright CP (2010) The Impact of TLS on SIP Server Performance. In: Proceedings of the 4th Annual ACM Conference on Principles, Systems and Applications of IP Telecommunications (IPTCOMM), pp 63–74

[230] Sher M, Magedanz T (2007) Protecting IP Multimedia Subsystem (IMS) Service Delivery Platform from Time Independent Attacks. In: Proceedings of the 3rd International Symposium on Information Assurance and Security (IAS), pp 171–176

[231] Shin D, Shim C (2005) Voice Spam Control with Gray Leveling. In: Proceedings of the 2nd VoIP Security Workshop

[232] Shin D, Ahn J, Shim C (2006) Progressive Multi Gray-Leveling: A Voice Spam Protection Algorithm. IEEE Network 20(5):18–24

[233] Sicker D, Lookabaugh T (2004) VoIP Security: Not an Afterthought. ACM Queue Magazine 2(6):56–64

[234] Sijben P, van Willigenburg W, de Boer M, van der Gaast S (2002) Middleboxes: Controllable Media Firewalls. Bell Labs Technical Journal 7(1):141–157

[235] Singh K, Vuong S (2004) Blaze: A Mobile Agent Paradigm for VoIP Intrusion Detection Systems. In: Proceedings of the 1st International Conference on E-Business and Telecommunication Networks (ICETE)

[236] Singhai R, Sahoo A (2006) VoIP Security. Technical report, Indian Institute of Technology, Mumbai — School of Information Technology

[237] Sisalem D, Ehlert S, Geneiatakis D, Kambourakis G, Dagiuklas T, Markl J, Rokos M, Botron O, Rodriguez J, Liu J (2005) Towards a Secure and Reliable VoIP Infrastructure. Tech. Rep. Deliverable D2.1, SNOCER COOP-005892

[238] Sisalem D, Kuthan J, Ehlert S (2006) Denial of Service Attacks Targeting a SIP VoIP Infrastructure: Attack Scenarios and Prevention Mechanisms. IEEE Network 20(5):26–31

[239] Sisalem D, Floroiu J, Kuthan J, Abend U, Schulzrinne H (2009) SIP Security. Wiley

[240] Sollins K (1992) The TFTP Protocol (Revision 2). RFC 1350 (Standard), URL http://www.ietf.org/rfc/rfc1350.txt, updated by RFCs 1782, 1783, 1784, 1785, 2347, 2348, 2349

[241] Sorge C, Seedorf J (2009) A Provider-Level Reputation System for Assessing the Quality of SPIT Mitigation Algorithms. In: Proceedings of the IEEE Internation Conference on Communications (ICC), pp 1–6

[242] Soupionis Y, Dritsas S, Gritzalis D (2008) An Adaptive Policy-Based Approach to SPIT Management. In: Proceedings of the 13th European Symposium on Research in Computer Security (ESORICS), pp 446–460

[243] Sparks R, Lawrence S, Hawrylyshen A, Campen B (2008) Addressing an Amplification Vulnerability in Session Initiation Protocol (SIP) Forking Proxies. RFC 5393 (Proposed Standard), URL http://www.ietf.org/rfc/rfc5393.txt

[244] Srinivasan R, Vaidehi V, Harish K, Narasimhan KL, Babu SL, Srikanth V (2005) Authentication of Signaling in VoIP Applications. In: Proceedings of the 11th Asia-Pacific Conference on Communications (APCC), pp 530–533

[245] Srisuresh P, Egevang K (2001) Traditional IP Network Address Translator (Traditional NAT). RFC 3022 (Informational), URL http://www.ietf.org/rfc/rfc3022.txt

[246] Srivastava K, Schulzrinne H (2004) Preventing Spam For SIP-based Instant Messages and Sessions. Technical Report CUCS-042-04, Columbia University, Department of Computer Science

[247] Srivatsa M, Liu L, Iyengar A (2008) Preserving Caller Anonymity in Voice-over-IP Networks. In: Proceedings of the IEEE Symposium on Security and Privacy (S&P), pp 50–63

[248] Srivatsa M, Iyengar A, Liu L (2009) Privacy in VoIP networks: A k-Anonymity Approach. In: Proceedings of the 28th IEEE Conference on Computer Communication (INFOCOM), pp 2856–2860

[249] State R, Festor O, Abdelanur H, Pascual V, Kuthan J, Coeffic R, Janak J, Floroiu J (2009) SIP digest authentication relay attack. draft-state-sip-relay-attack-00, URL http://tools.ietf.org/html/draft-state-sip-relay-attack-00

[250] Steinebach M, Siebenhaar F, Neubauer C, Ackermann R, Roedig U, Dittmann J (2002) Intrusion Detection Systems for IP Telephony Networks. In: Proceedings of the Real Time Intrusion Detection Symposium, pp 1–9

[251] Stott DT (2005) SAFENeT: Server-based Architecture For Enterprise NAT and Firewall Traversal. In: Proceedings of the 2nd VoIP Security Workshop

[252] Takahashi T, Lee W (2007) An Assessment of VoIP Covert Channel Threats. In: Proceedings off the 3rd International Conference on Security and Privacy in Communications Networks (SecureComm), pp 371–380

[253] Talevski A, Chang E, Dillon T (2007) Secure Mobile VoIP. In: Proceedings of the International Conference on Convergence Information Technology, pp 2108–2113

[254] Tang J, Cheng Y, Zhou C (2009) Sketch-based SIP Flooding Detection Using Hellinger Distance. In: Proceedings of the IEEE Global Telecommunications Conference (GLOBECOM), pp 1–6

[255] The Register (2006) Two charged with VoIP fraud. `http://www.theregister.co.uk/2006/06/08/voip_fraudsters_nabbed/`

[256] The Register (2009) Fugitive VOIP hacker cuffed in Mexico. `http://www.theregister.co.uk/2009/02/11/fugitive_voip_hacker_arrested/`

[257] Thermos P, Hadsall G (2005) Vulnerabilities in SOHO VoIP Gateways. In: Proceedings of the 2nd VoIP Security Workshop

[258] Thermos P, Takanen A (2008) Securing VoIP Networks. Pearson Education

[259] Truong P, Nieh D, Moh M (2005) Specification-based Intrusion Detection for H.323-based Voice over IP. In: Proceedings of the IEEE International Symposium on Signal Processing and Information Technology

[260] Tsai JL (2009) Efficient Nonce-based Authentication Scheme for Session Initiation Protocol. International Journal of Network Security (IJNS) 9(1):12–16

[261] Tschofenig H, Falk R, Peterson J, Hodges J, Sicker D, Polk J (2006) Using SAML to Protect the Session Initiation Protocol (SIP). IEEE Network 20(5):14–17

[262] Tucker GS (2005) Voice Over Internet Protocol (VoIP) and Security. White paper, SANS Institute

[263] Verscheure O, Vlachos M, Anagnostopoulos A, Frossard P, Bouillet E, Yu PS (2006) Finding "who is talking to whom" in VoIP Networks via Progressive Stream Clustering. In: Proceedings of the 6th International Conference on Data Mining (ICDM), p 667=677

[264] VoIP Security Alliance (2005) VoIP Security and Privacy Threat Taxonomy, version 1.0. `http://www.voipsa.org/Activities/taxonomy.php`

[265] Vuong S, Bai Y (2004) A Survey of VoIP Intrusions and Intrusion Detection Systems. In: Proceedings of the 6th International Conference on Advanced Communication Technology (ICACT), pp 317–322

[266] Walsh TJ, Kuhn DR (2005) Challenges in Securing Voice over IP. IEEE Security & Privacy Magazine 3(3):44–49

[267] Wang CH, Li MW, Liao W (2007) A Distributed Key-Changing Mechanism for Secure Voice over IP (VoIP) Service. In: Proceedings of the IEEE International Conference on Multimedia and Expo, pp 895–898

[268] Wang F, Zhang Y (2008) A New Provably Secure Authentication and Key Agreement for SIP Using Certificateless Public-Key Cryptography. Computer Communications 31(10):2142–2149

[269] Wang T (2007) A VoIP anti-Spam System based on Reverse Turing Test. Masters Thesis ETD-05072007-173147, North Carolina State University

[270] Wang X, Zhang R, Yang X, Jiang X, Wijesekera D (2008) Voice Pharming Attack and the Trust of VoIP. In: Proceedings of the 4th International Conference on Security and Privacy in Communication Networks (SecureComm), pp 1–11

[271] Wieser C, Laakso M, Schulzrinne H (2003) Security Testing of SIP Implementations. Tech. Rep. CUCS-024-03, Columbia University, Department of Computer Science

[272] Wieser C, Röning J, Takanen A (2006) Security analysis and experiments for Voice over IP RTP media streams. In: Proceedings of the 8th International Symposium on Systems and Information Security (SSI)

[273] Wright CV, Ballard L, Monrose FN, Masson GM (2007) Language Identification of Encrypted VoIP Traffic: Alejandra y Roberto or Alice and Bob? In: Proceedings of 16th USENIX Security Symposium, pp 1–12

[274] Wright CV, Ballard L, Coulls S, Monrose FN, Masson GM (2008) Spot Me If You Can: Recovering Spoken Phrases in Encrypted VoIP Conversations. In: Proceedings of IEEE Symposium on Security and Privacy, pp 35–49

[275] Wu Y, Bagchi S, Garg S, Singh N (2004) SCIDIVE: A Stateful and Cross Protocol Intrusion Detection Architecture for Voice-over-IP Environments. In: Proceedings of the Conference on Dependable Systems and Networks (DSN, pp 433–442

[276] Wu YS, Apte V, Bagchi S, Garg S, Singh N (2009) Intrusion Detection in Voice over IP Environments. International Journal of Information Security 8(3):153–172

[277] Wu YS, Bagchi S, Singh N, Wita R (2009) Spam Detection in Voice-Over-IP Calls through Semi-Supervised Clustering. In: Proceedings of the 39th Annual IEEE/IFIP International Conference on Dependable Systems and Networks (DSN), pp 307–316

[278] Xiao H, Zarrella P (2004) Quality Effects of Wireless VoIP Using Security Solutions. In: Proceedings of the IEEE Military Communications Conference (MILCOM), vol 3, pp 1352–1357

[279] Xin J (2007) Security Issues and Countermeasure for VoIP . White paper, SANS Institute

[280] XWang, Chen S, Jajodia S (2005) Tracking Anonymous Peer-to-Peer VoIP Calls on the Internet. In: Proceedings of the 12th ACM Conference on Computer and Communications Security (CCS), pp 81–91

[281] Yan H, Zhang H, Sripanidkulchai K, Shae Z, Saha D (2006) Incorporating Active Fingerprinting into SPIT Prevention Systems. In: Proceedings of the 3rd Workshop on Securing Voice over IP

[282] Yang CC, Wang RC, Liu WT (2005) Secure Authentication Scheme for Session Initiation Protocol. Computers and Security 24(5):381–386

[283] Yoon EJ, Yoo KY (2009) A New Authentication Scheme for Session Initiation Protocol. In: Proceedings of the International Conference on Complex, Intelligent and Software Intensive Systems, pp 549–554

[284] Zandi M, Martin MV, Hung PCK (2007) Overview of Security Issues of VOIP. In: Proceedings of the IASTED European Conference on Internet and Multimedia Systems and Applications (IMSA), pp 254–259

[285] Zave P (2008) Understanding SIP Through Model-Checking. In: Proceedings of the 2nd International Conference on Principles, Systems and Applications of IP Telecommunications (IPTComm), pp 256–279

[286] Zhang G, Berthold S (2010) Hidden VoIP Calling Records from Networking Intermediaries. In: Proceedings of the 4th Annual ACM Conference on Principles, Systems and Applications of IP Telecommunications (IPTCOMM), pp 15–24

[287] Zhang G, Fischer-Hübner S (2010) Peer-to-Peer VoIP Communications Using Anonymisation Overlay Networks. In: Proceedings of the 11th Conference on Communications and Multimedia Security (CMS)

[288] Zhang G, Ehlert S, Magedanz T, Sisalem D (2007) Denial of Service Attack and Prevention on SIP VoIP Infrastructures Using DNS Flooding. In: Proceedings of the 1st International Conference on Principles, Systems and Applications of IP Telecommunications (IPTCOMM), pp 57–66

[289] Zhang R, Wang X, Yang X, Jiang X (2007) Billing Attacks on SIP-based VoIP Systems. In: Proceedings of the 1st USENIX Workshop On Offensive Technologies (WOOT), pp 1–8

[290] Zhang R, Wang X, Farley R, Yang X, Jiang X (2009) On the Feasibility of Launching the Man-In-The-Middle Attacks on VoIP from Remote Attackers. In: Proceedings of the 4th International ACM Symposium on Information, Computer, and Communications Security (ASIACCS), pp 61–69